A
MARINE'S
DAUGHTER

A
MARINE'S
DAUGHTER

AL HAGUE

gatekeeper press

Columbus, Ohio

This book is a work of fiction. The names, characters and events in this book are the products of the author's imagination or are used fictitiously. Any similarity to real persons living or dead is coincidental and not intended by the author.

A Marine's Daughter

Published by Gatekeeper Press
2167 Stringtown Rd, Suite 109
Columbus, OH 43123-2989
www.GatekeeperPress.com

Copyright © 2018 by Al Hague
All rights reserved. Neither this book, nor any parts within it may be sold or reproduced in any form or by any electronic or mechanical means, including information storage and retrieval systems without permission in writing from the author. The only exception is by a reviewer, who may quote short excerpts in a review.

ISBN (hardcover): 9781642371185
ISBN (paperback): 9781642374643
eISBN: 9781642371338

Printed in the United States of America

CONTENTS

DEDICATION

AMarine's Daughter is dedicated to the thousands of men and women who served their country past and present. The sacrifice made by so many throughout history must never be forgotten. To those men and women in all the branches of the military who did their duty and came home to live the best life they could for their family and themselves, we as a country owe ongoing support and gratitude.

THE MARINE'S PRAYER

Almighty Father, whose command is over all and whose love never fails, make me aware of Thy presence and obedient to Thy will. Keep me true to my best self, guarding me against dishonesty in purpose and deed and helping me to live so that I can face my fellow Marines, my loved ones and Thee without shame or fear. Protect my family. Give me the will to do the work of a Marine and to accept my share of responsibilities with vigor and enthusiasm. Grant me the courage to be proficient in my daily performance. Keep me loyal and faithful to my superiors and to the duties my country and the Marine Corps have entrusted to me. Make me considerate of those committed to my leadership. Help me to wear my uniform with dignity, and let it remind me daily of the traditions which I must uphold.

If I am inclined to doubt, steady my faith; if I am tempted, make me strong to resist; if I should miss the mark, give me courage to try again.

Guide me with the light of truth and grant me wisdom by which I may understand the answer to my prayer.

Amen

CHAPTER ONE

The years had been kind to Sgt. Jon Milo, at least in outward appearance. He was tall, and walked and sat with good posture learned long ago. He still had a full head of hair and as yet had avoided a gut that would prevent him from seeing his belt buckle. His physique for a man his age –in fact for most any age– revealed his lifestyle had been one of hard physical work and few vices.

A life spent working with his hands in construction gave him strength. His desire to take care of himself so he could be there for his wonderful daughter long term had kept him on as healthy a path as possible. Losing his beautiful wife at such a young age was enough to knock most men to the ground but Jon controlled his grief in order to provide for his daughter, Sara Jane. The difficult issue of letting go continued to haunt Jon. He had never shown any interest in seeking out another relationship after he lost Serena. He knew deep down that this would be very disappointing to her that he had never been able to move on. Perhaps the time was here to let himself enjoy the art of appreciating the female species. He was certain that Serena would want him to find some happiness and not be afraid of giving of himself to someone. He made a mental note to work on that and to do it soon.

On the inside he suffered immensely. He often felt like a man many years his senior. The effects of Agent Orange were taking their toll and his battle with his health was a daily struggle. Most likely was only going to get worse.

Tonight was one of those nights when he really did not have anything to keep his mind occupied and after fixing himself a meager dinner of hot dogs and beans, his thoughts wandered to years ago. No doubt it was the story about a young Marine who had earned the Medal of Honor in Iraq, which he saw on television this evening. The story of a hero brought back the nagging fear that had plagued Jon every day since he was wounded. He still did not know for certain if he had let his men down or not. He still needed to know that answer.

Jon remembered lying in his hospital bed in California healing from his wounds watching the hippie protests on television denouncing not only the war, but also the thousands of young men and women who were doing the fighting every day. The painful memories of those days were perhaps the worst part of the return from that hellhole called South Viet Nam.

He recalled how he felt obligated to join in the protests but his loyalty to the men he left behind would not allow that choice. His guilt for taking part in the war tormented him then and all the years since.

Over the years he had often wondered if he would ever be able to forgive his country for the way all of the Vets were treated upon their return during his time. He knew down deep that he sometimes even felt jealous about today's warriors and the recognition and love that were shown to them by his country. Even the anti-war segment of the population seems to hold veterans in esteem these days.

Jon sat in his old chair and stared into the fireplace. He suddenly realized the fire was almost out. Jon knew these thoughts were coming more frequently and he was quite sure it was not a coincidence that his recollections and dreams had grown more regular since he had retired.

"Perhaps it's just that I don't have much else on my mind anymore," he said aloud.

Snapping out of the past and into the future Jon reminded himself that Christmas was almost here and his beautiful daughter would be visiting for the holiday. *I have a lot to do to get ready for Sara, so enough of this daydreaming about the past.* Turning out the lights and heading down the hall he caught himself, about to say goodnight to Serena, his beautiful bride. No matter how many years she'd been gone he somehow always sensed her still at his side.

CHAPTER TWO

Winter was well at work as Sara left the church on Wednesday evening, just one week before Christmas. The choir and organist offered the most soothing and reverent music of the season. The tall carved and imposing mahogany doors of the magnificent cathedral opened to the outside and she was immediately breathless with the beauty of the night before her. Her solo annual holiday celebration began years before and only over the past few seasons did she find enjoyment at many local churches. On this night, it was St. Patrick's Cathedral.

The magnificent well-known structure with its Gothic Revival architecture was prominent amongst the other New York City landmarks. Each step Sara took matched the tempo of her favorite holiday song. She hummed the music and heard the words in her mind...
'Silent Night, Holy Night, all is Calm, all is Bright.'

Singing the favorite Christmas melody had always been a tradition for Sara and an integral part of the memories easily recalled from her happy childhood times with her Mom and Dad.

Of course for pure holiday inspiration this time of year nothing could compare to Rockefeller Center. Its abundance of opulent Christmas decorations of all shapes and sizes, and the ice rink, indeed a special place where so many young couples gathered to show off their skating skills. The ambiance even lent itself as a special place for young lovers to get on bended knee to pop the question. Some would make the evening sojourn through the hectic holiday streets just to enjoy a hot chocolate, often spiked with something stronger from a personal flask hidden in their coat.

Each season Sara would remind herself to make time to visit Radio City Music Hall for the perennial Christmas show. This year her alone time was running out for the season. She would soon be leaving to spend this holiday with her dad in their family home, back in her small hometown in Massachusetts.

Tonight the snow was falling ever so gently. Each flake offered a slow-motion effect in a collective density shimmering from the lone streetlight at the corners of 5th Avenue and 53rd Street. The only sound was the slight squeak of her footsteps as she walked along the sidewalk away from the church. It was a moment that required no words of any kind.

Sara wanted to just take it all in as this was undoubtedly a "Silent Night" to appreciate and remember. She couldn't't help wonder where are all the horns, the traffic, the noises of the city that never sleeps were. *It just can't be this quiet*, she thought. She walked along with the snowflakes touching her face and for Sara they felt a bit like tears. Sara usually would only think of her father in the present, but her thoughts on this night were about her mom from the past. How she missed her, particularly at holiday time. Sara began to think about what was happening in her life and at the moment the most important person in her life, her dad, was foremost in her thoughts on this peaceful but chilly night. She had become very concerned about his health lately. After all, he was getting on in years, even if he did resist grasping that reality. Sara also thought about the struggle she was involved in, on behalf of her father. It seemed like it had been such a long battle and sadly she did not hold out a lot of hope to be able to put together all of the details and testimonies required to build a case for what she felt was long overdue.

Her thoughts raced back to a special moment in time, so long ago, when she was walking with her dad outside the church. It was just after they had said goodbye to her mom and while they were certainly close there was some distance created by their individual grief.

The Christmas holiday this year seemed to take on more meaning. Perhaps it was because Sara was feeling somewhat alone. Not knowing the details of her father's health didn't help. She knew she would have to make the effort to know and understand. He was very good at keeping things to himself. She knew it was his way of protecting her.

Sara heard the bells from the church or at least she thought they were bells. As she awakened she realized it was just her alarm pulling into a new day. Climbing out of bed she thought that dream seemed so real. As she recalled the details she knew that much of it had actually happened. *Very strange*, she thought, but did not have time to dwell on it this morning.

Sara Milo a somewhat tall, leggy woman, with chestnut colored hair, brown eyes and lips that must have been designed by some lipstick manufacturer. She was strikingly beautiful, with a svelte figure that she could only attribute to good family genes, most likely from her mother. Sara had never had any problem with suitors, but she also had very high standards. She often wondered if she had measured the men in her life by what she saw in her father. Of course, her hectic professional life as a lawyer may have scared some men away. Or perhaps she was merely waiting for her dream man.

As she stepped into the shower, she thought maybe today would be the day she would hear from the Marine Corps or her Congressman's office regarding her request for her father's case to be investigated. She had jumped through all the hoops required to get her dad what she thought he deserved. But with each passing year, much of the evidence proving his actions was long gone or was among many of the missing records of that time.

Finishing her shower, she glanced at her watch and realized her daydreaming would make her a bit late leaving for the office. The city traffic would be also be slower after last night's snow. The morning after a snowfall was always an adventure when taking a taxi; the treacherous streets could make for a scary ride. No time to make her morning coffee, she hoped there would be some left at the office. With a bit of luck and a short quick text to her assistant Victoria she would have her morning starter at her desk.

Her day would be very full with last minute papers and filings before the long weekend. Christmas on a Thursday or Friday always presented problems with courts closing and the senior partners taking time off, unlike the junior partners who couldn't afford to.

It was days like this Sara was glad she did not own a car in Manhattan. Parking alone was impossible, not to mention the hazardous winter conditions, dodging taxis and people texting or talking on their phones.

Part of the reason for long hours was the insane competition between junior partners, and occasionally even the associates who planned on climbing the ladder in the office hierarchy. One junior in particular, Stefan Wood, had joined the firm at the same time as Sara and he was, in her mind, a first class jackass. His stuffed shirt demeanor and ass kissing habits often rubbed her and the other junior partners the wrong way. He had talent but nowhere near as much as he thought he had. Yet somehow he usually managed to get lowly associates to do much of the grunt work that he should have been doing himself.

He tried to use intimidation to get what he wanted and often it worked, but Sara was not having any of his bullshit. Over time they were anything but friends and because of her record in court and perhaps even her looks, Stefan did his best to stay out of her way. *Today had better not be an exception*, Sarah thought to herself as her mind was still on her dream. *How do I reach Dad without making him feel that I am being bossy?* Sara arrived in her comfortable but small office on time, and her assistant Victoria had her coffee ready with a smile and a warm greeting:

"Good Morning Boss." Sara did not like being called boss but let Victoria get away with a lot just because she was a fantastic assistant. She was always on time, never missed a deadline. Whenever Sara needed to focus on her work, Victoria would deflect any unnecessary intrusions or distractions, allowing Sara to be single-minded. Plus her legal knowledge was on par with many of the associates. She just did not have the degree, yet.

To date, Sara had not shared her tilting at the military windmill with her, but she did not doubt that soon she might need her assistant's advice. Victoria was an on the edge girl, not only the way she dressed but also in her conversations as she did not suffer fools very well. Today must be a big day for some reason as Vickie, decked out in a beautiful sweater and skirt with heels, looked much more conservative than usual. Sara was impressed that Vic had even reduced the visible cleavage considerably.

No doubt there are several men around that will be disappointed today, she thought. The good news was for one reason or another, perhaps many, Victoria was very loyal to Sara and Sara knew she could count on her not only for the quality of work but also discretion when required.

Sitting down Sara asked, "What time is my first conference?"

Vickie replied with a smirk, "About five minutes ago."

"Oh crap, why didn't you say something?" Sara said as she jumped to her feet, grabbed the file and headed for the door.

"I would have, but you're fine. It's just another meeting with Mr. Childs, and he's always late, so chill girl, and take your coffee," Victoria assured Sara.

CHAPTER THREE

I t was a hot and nasty day on the barren, dry and dirty hill about 5 clicks northwest of the airbase at Da Nang, South Viet Nam. Even with the presumed cooler air from the Gulf of Tonkin, an important armpit of the South China Sea, it was stifling and insufferable. Corporal Jonathan Milo, for now an FNG (fucking new guy), sat on a stack of sandbags, writing a letter back home to his family, letting them know that he arrived safely a few days ago.

Writing a letter in such conditions was not easy. Jon fought against the sweat dripping off his forehead and onto his paper, smearing the ink. Chuckling to himself, he wondered if his mother might believe the ink was messed up from tears falling on the paper. He had to make sure she knew it was sweat. *Damn it's hot and sticky! The humidity is so bad your clothes soak through in minutes every morning.* Nighttime didn't't bring much relief either.

His actual arrival date was April 5, 1966, and he became part of the 3rd Marine Amphibious Force. Jon had been in the Marine Corps since 1964 and was a very squared away Marine, earning the rank of E-4 rather quickly by Marine Corps standards. He was stationed at Camp Lejeune when the Corps cut his orders to Okinawa. Jon, as his friends and family called him, was a tall guy about 6' 2", very rugged and in shape at 185 pounds, at least for the time being. His rugged good looks and quiet, confident manner had served him well in the Corps, and he had always led by example.

If he had one fault, it was his undying devotion to whatever the Corps and his government leaders directed him to do. His kind of dedication and unwavering commitment was required to be a leader and to set an example for those young men he led every day. Viet Nam was his first combat assignment, except for a short time quelling a civil war in Central America when he was with the 6th Marines at Camp LeJeune. Now his unit's task was to protect the Da Nang Airbase from the Viet Cong.

Marine Corps units were spread around the base, forming a perimeter of Marines that would be required to not only guard the base's perimeter, but also to conduct search and destroy missions and engage the enemy. As a squad leader, Jon was responsible for the organizing, training, and the individual assignments of his squad of twelve men. Often the squad, which was part of a platoon of about fifty, was reinforced by a weapons team with mortars and automatic weapons, depending on the mission. At the young age of 24, Jon had an enormous responsibility not only to his men but also to his officers. Scuttlebutt (gossip) was saying the platoon would be part of a major operation soon and it was a fact in the Marine Corps that scuttlebutt was never wrong. Well, almost never, it depended on one's point of view. The smart way was not to believe anything until the orders came through the chain of command. Jon checked his watch and realized he needed to get his ass over to the company bunker to meet with his platoon Sargent and get his squads assignments for the night. If the assignments were as usual his squad would have the tough end spot of the line. That meant his people had to pay attention forward as well as to their left flank. He often wondered, as did his men, why they were always chosen to have the tough job. During the past weeks, the young troops had been digging all the foxholes and filling thousands of sandbags necessary to reinforce the positions along the main line of defense. Fields of fire stakes had been installed to limit the direction the machine guns could point to prevent men firing at night in the wrong direction. The stakes were set to create intersecting lines of fire, thus making penetration of the lines much more impossible for Charlie.

Extra defensive posts were necessary because not every post was manned every night as Charlie (Viet Cong) had eyes everywhere and would often probe the lines trying to find out which positions were being used. Perimeter guard was a tough assignment; complete silence was a requirement and staying awake throughout the night critical. Most foxholes had two men each, one awake and one sleeping, usually in two-hour shifts.

The nights were long in the jungle. When the rain came, it seemed to last forever. Everything was wet, and the bugs, the damn bugs, as every Marine in the Nam could attest, should have had wing numbers painted on them. They were big and they were plentiful.

The bugs and the rain were the physical irritants, but it was the effect on the mind that took the real toll. The noises heard that couldn't be identified, the shadows one could swear were moving, and in some cases, they were. And then there was the darkness and the fear of the unknown or fear of the things conjured in one's mind.

The granddaddy of them all for Jon, the fear that he would let the other men down in some fashion when the shit hit the fan. Every Marine in this place was doing his best to survive and see that the guy next to him survived as well. In the foxholes no one discussed the politics of the situation, only the best way to survive and get back to "the world."

For a leader like Jon that fear and desire was multiplied many times. The responsibility he felt was like an elephant sitting on his shoulders and his concern for his men was his guiding beacon. Everything he did was with their best interest in mind, whether it was getting hot chow for everyone or making sure each man had his equipment in perfect shape or looking after their physical health. He tended to put himself last. Often he played the part of a chaplain, listening to the problems of his men, which ranged from fear to bad news from home.

During the night on the line he quietly traveled to each foxhole, checking on the men and making sure someone was awake in every hole. If and when they got hit by Charlie, the line had to hold, and the intersecting lines of fire were the only way not to have holes in the perimeter and allow Charlie to overrun their positions.

The night passed ever so slowly, and as the sun rose, the platoon was relieved and exhausted as they packed up their gear and headed back to base camp. Much of the exhaustion came from the mental torture and intense concentration required to get through the night. It was incredible how staying completely silent took so much energy. Each man was responsible for making sure he left no trace behind for Charlie to find. Leaving anything behind could have Charlie waiting for them the next time they used this area. It was a matter of life and death to avoid being predictable, and every man knew that only too well.

First things first, almost to a man, each lit a cigarette, a habit impossible to break in this miserable place. The quiet nights, personal silence and awareness of their dubious position only exacerbated their need to indulge. Of course it seemed that half the team bummed a cigarette from the other half, which always led to some good-natured bitching. But then a good Marine was not happy unless he was bitching about something. As he led his men to the rear, he allowed himself to think a bit about home. After listening to the plight of some of his men he was grateful he did not leave anyone behind except his family. Jon was convinced that he was too young to get tied down and besides, while he was at Camp Lejeune, it was obvious to him that women in general liked men in uniform. Of course, he was young compared to others but given that most of his men were between 17 and 20, at 24 he was by their thinking, an old man.

One of his young Marines was a bit of a "wise guy" from New Jersey. Of course with the last name like Roselli, he could be a true "wise guy" but not likely. He was simply a kid from Jersey who had a strange sense of humor. He was also ruggedly good-looking, with sometimes-curly hair and a large wide smile. With all of this, he was still a good Marine. As they approached the camp, Roselli yelled out, "Hey Corporal, can we get something to eat besides C Rats tonight?"

"Only if you cook it, Roselli." Roselli's family owned an Italian restaurant in Union, NJ, and that is about all the kid ever talked about was food. Food and the women he claimed to have dated, tales that no one believed.

"Corporal, you and these bums should be so lucky to have me cook for you," Roselli wisecracked. "You would ask me to marry you."

Somewhere in the distance, Jon could hear an obnoxious ringing. The sound came closer and as he shook himself from the fitful sleep he thought, *would these fucking dreams ever stop? It's like a broken record, over and over.*

"I need some coffee," Jon said aloud as he climbed out of bed. *Right after I take these damn pills,* he thought, reaching for the pillbox he had sitting next to his bed. Each morning while taking the pills he wondered if all these chemicals the VA was giving him were doing more harm than good.

CHAPTER FOUR

It was only three days to Christmas and today was a long day for Sara. Hours waiting in court and then getting yelled at by a judge did not make for a banner day but all in all, she accomplished most of what she had on her schedule, and now it was time for sleep. As she lay there, her mind went back to the beginning of this quest to get her father his due before it was too late.

Dad had returned from Viet Nam before he and her mother had even met, so her recollection of him did not include much of anything about Viet Nam. As she was growing up, she knew he had been in the war and always had a feeling he was living with some bad memories, but like most of the men of those times, he never talked about his experiences.

As curious as Sara was she managed to keep her curiosity to herself all while growing up. Dad has always provided well for the family with his small but successful construction business in Massachusetts. He had been a loving and supportive father. He made sacrifices to help her through law school, and those sacrifices did not go unnoticed. Her dad drove a ten-year-old car and rarely bought himself much of anything. Her mom had died when Sara was just thirteen so for years it was just she and her dad.

About a year ago a letter came addressed to Sara from a gentleman by the name of Dominic Roselli. The contents revealed that for many years now men from her Dad's old outfit had been trying to reach him and he had always ignored the communications. As was his style, he did not mention anything about it to his daughter. This time they looked for and found Sara with Google and contacted her to determine if she would talk to them about her dad.

A telephone call followed the letter, and the conversation was a startling revelation to Sara. Dominic told her a story of her Dad's heroism that had gone entirely unrecognized all these many years. It turned out there were several men dedicated to making that right, assuming she would help them.

The description talked about his selfless act in a firefight that saved several men from being killed, and he did all of it while having no regard for his own safety. For one reason or another, there was no record of the battle at the time, but perhaps with the detailed testimony and recollection of several of his men, Jon would finally receive the honor he so well deserved. The challenge was going to be the politics and the red tape, but also how to go about it without her dad's knowledge; they were all concerned that he might resist the recognition.

"Mr. Roselli, I am speechless, I had no idea that any of what you are telling me even happened. I don't know what to say."

" I understand how much of a shock this must be for you, but we need your help," said Roselli. Not only because you are Sergeant Jon's daughter but also because you are a lawyer and, well, that is what it is going to take. We have done some of the necessary research and can send you what we have if you like."

"Dominic, thank you but I need a bit of time to digest all of this, and I don't want to upset Dad with making him uncomfortable in any way. Most importantly if it turns out to be something he would like and appreciate I wouldn't want to disappoint him. May I get back to you in a few days?" Sara asked.

"Yes of course, Sara. How is he doing anyway?"

"He's doing okay. As you probably know, Agent Orange affected him, like so many of you. He is getting the support and medical help at the VA, and thankfully his mood is usually good. He keeps as busy as he can with projects and helping people, which I guess is his nature, just as it always has been. I am concerned about his health of course, and I also suspect he's not telling me everything. I also think his old wounds bother him more than he lets on, and I worry about complications with all of that. He won't let me go to the VA with him, and when I ask about his appointments, I get the usual 'nothing new.' It is difficult with the miles between us but I am spending Christmas with him, and I hope to learn for myself more of what is really happening." Sara explained.

"I understand and thank you. You should decide if you want to share our plan with him or not and if so when. I will wait for your call," said Dominic.

"Mr. Roselli, may I ask, how are you? I assume you are suffering many of the same issues as my dad?"

"Yes Sara, we are all pretty much in the same boat. I am one of the lucky ones. I managed to not get my ass shot off and that is because of your father. He saved many of us more than once," Roselli said, plainly grateful.

"One of the guys is not doing well at all and he really wants to have the chance to thank the Sarge if at all possible. It has been weighing on all of us for far too long. I'm not surprised your dad hasn't reached out to anyone but maybe he will let us reach out to him. Please keep in touch and let us know what we can do. Please Sara," Dominic asked sincerely.

"Yes Dominic. I'll do what I can and I promise you I will be in touch. I'll look for your statements in the mail that I can use to try to make something happen. I do have a few connections that might be helpful or can at least point me in the right direction."

That was the beginning of all of this "extracurricular activity" and although only a year had passed by, it seemed much longer. In the first month after the Roselli conversation, Sara started the ball rolling by reaching out to her Congressman's office. She had never met him, but he had a reputation for supporting veteran causes, so she felt he was an excellent place to start.

Waiting every day for news from Congressman Platt's office was frustrating. *I need to call them again soon,* she thought as she turned out the light. *Perhaps I'll find a way to meet the Congressman and make my plea in person.* As she closed her eyes her mind carried her back to the dream she had about leaving the Cathedral, and it was at that moment in recalling the words of 'Silent Night' she thought to herself, *I'm not sure I ever paid attention to the words. I was always so focused on the notes and the sound of the choir. Maybe I need to start paying attention more to words in my personal life and not just the music.*

As a lawyer, I make my living with words, but in my personal life, all I hear are the notes. That can't be good, she thought. It was getting late, and Sara considered taking a sedative to sleep well, but she also felt the little pills caused her to dream and she needed a good night's sleep. She was expecting a busy day tomorrow. Three days until she headed to Massachusetts to see her dad.

CHAPTER FIVE

Jon was in the waiting room at the VA to meet with his doctor, who wanted him to have some more tests. The last tests had not been very encouraging. Whatever it was he would deal with it. It was Sara he was more concerned about at the moment. Sitting there deep in thought, he watched as a young man in a wheelchair came by with an attendant helping him down the corridor. Memories of his time on the hospital ship off the coast of Da Nang came flooding back. His wounds had been severe but not life threatening. He was being well treated and cared for but try as he might; he had no recall of the events that put him there.

All Jon could remember was being on patrol, and tracers were everywhere. He recalled some of his men screaming at him for instructions and direction, and then he did what he was trained to do. All he ever thought about was if he had failed his men. He would like an answer to that nagging question. He never went back to his unit.

He was sent home to a stateside hospital straight from the hospital ship for recovery. Over time he tried to learn what had happened, but he always got the same answers; the people who knew what happened were still "in country" and he would have to be patient.

It was during this time in the hospital that the anger took control of him. He was disgusted with the government that sent so many men like himself to that hell, that quagmire. While he was in the hospital the television screen showed either newsreels from the war or news coverage of the protests and riots. Both made him sick in many ways. As he healed and was able to go home, he began staying out of the world as much as possible. Little by little, through conversations with his father, who had been in WWII, he learned how to put the terror and sadness behind him and move on.

That is indeed the short version, he thought to himself. The volunteer at the desk called out his name and sent him to the examining room to meet with his doctor. *This appointment should be interesting* he, thought nervously. As time went by he reminded himself that it was time to be social if the opportunity presented. He really needs to pay attention to attractive women once again, he was sure he could hear Serena saying in his head.

After sitting in the examining room for what seemed an eternity the door finally slid back and in walked a woman with the usual stethoscope around her neck, and Jon couldn't help notice what a lovely neck it was. He thought to himself, *where the hell did she come from and why did she leave wherever it was?* She was tall with reddish brown hair and a body to stop traffic. Her eyes as she said hello sparkled like a well-lit Christmas tree. *Now that is a corny bunch of thinking, but it's honest. What happened to Dr. Cardoza?*

"Good Morning Mr. Milo, my name is Dr. Stewart, and I am now your doctor. Dr. Cardoza transferred to a different facility a week ago. I hope you are okay with this change. If you prefer to have a male doctor, I do understand," she said.

Jon was speechless and a bit shocked as he thought to himself, *how the hell did I get this lucky?*

"Dr. Stewart I have no issue with a change. No offense but you are a lot easier on these old eyes than Doc Cardoza, so no…no problem," he admitted.

"Well, thank you," she responded. "I appreciate the compliment, but we have to get your tests scheduled. I have read your long history, and I must say you have done amazing all of these years with what you went through so long ago. But we need to deal with what we have today. According to the results of your last test, your kidneys are not doing all that well, and your blood pressure fluctuations have me very concerned. I would like to test again to see if there has been any change and then see you in a few days and go over the results with you. Are you comfortable with that?" she asked.

"Sure Doc, whatever you say," Jon said. At the same time he was thinking, *if only I were 30 years younger.*

Jon decided to take a chance. "Doc, can I ask you a question?"

"Of course," Doctor 'Lovely' replied. He had already put a nickname on her.

"I know you are a doctor and I also have eyes so in my mind you do not fit the VA mold." Jon blurted. Jon could sense this was perhaps a regular routine faced by Dr. Stewart, but it was worth the time just to feel flirtatious.

"No offense intended But I need to ask how and why did you come to work in a VA Hospital when you most likely could have any spot in the best hospital anywhere, any time?" Jon asked.

Dr. Lovely replied. "That's an easy question for me to answer. My father was a veteran, and he died just before I finished medical school. I made a commitment to myself to help and work for vets as long as I could, so here I am."

As she was leaving the office she put her hand on his shoulder. "I will see you next week Sgt. Milo."

For the first time Jon walked out of the VA Hospital with a smile on his face, feeling almost like a teenager. *What a day,* he thought to himself.

On the way home, he was thinking about Sara and how he had kept so much from her all these years, mainly because he never felt the time was right to share his secrets and struggles. He wanted to because he knew she was strong enough to handle all of it. When his time came, he did not want to leave her with questions that would haunt her into her old age, much as his father had done with him. He decided that if the reports were not favorable, he would tell her very soon. Hopefully, he could also find the right time to share his past with her. *It won't be a short story* he thought, *but she has a right to know, assuming she wants to know.* No matter what, he vowed to himself to let her in, finally.

The holidays would be in full force and with that time arrived the annual Christmas parties and in particular, the dreaded office party. Sara certainly had very little interest in dodging the advances of co-workers, but her absence would be conspicuous, so she had to gather up the determination to attend.

If I have to go to this mandated Christmas gathering, Sara thought to herself, *I might as well go all out and make a statement that will make a lasting impression.* As she recalled, quite often the senior partners invited many outsiders, which was their way to leverage influence and reinforce connections. *Maybe I'll get lucky and make a couple of contacts for myself.* With a bit of luck, she might connect with some Washington, DC types that could help her with her quest on behalf of her dad.

The party was Friday night, which meant she had one day to find the perfect dress and shoes that would show her off without seeming too flagrant. She wasn't sure why the mood to be so bold had come along, but it certainly did put a smile on her face, and it provided a sense of empowerment. *Being me sometimes has its moments*, she thought, followed by a wry smile meant to match her plans.

Arriving home, she went straight to her bedroom, which for many reasons she had never taken the time to really decorate. Being consumed with work and focused entirely on her career left little time to be interested in the world of fashion or decorating her home in any way. The apartment was indeed one that deserved serious attention but somehow it just was never a priority for Sara. Of the two bedrooms, one was empty. The pleasant enough kitchen would be better enjoyed by someone who cared about cooking. The living room that was intended to be the showplace of the home was sparse. *I used to enjoy cooking when I was with Dad as a teenager,* she mused. She recalled that he was so appreciative.

Maybe one day I will find that desire again when I have someone to cook for.

From the eighth floor looking down the river and out towards the New Jersey skyline on one end, the view of course was incredible. The other side offered a view of the night landscape of the city. Sara always appreciated the view, especially at night, and often wondered who was doing what at the moment she was looking out on the world around her. How many people were happy and enjoying life? How many were sad and lonely or in a relationship that wasn't healthy?

She was always glad she had not rushed into a relationship just for the sake of having one, only to be miserable and lonely even when not alone. She often wondered why she felt so strongly about romantic entanglements, particularly when as best she could remember she had great role models in her parents. Trying to make herself feel better, she reminded herself her life up to now had been all about her education and advancing in her career. Smiling, she also thought about her biological clock that was always running.

Ideally suited to entertaining it had been a long time since she had any visitors and the saddest part, she had never had a man visit her in her home. She thought to herself, *maybe I need to work on that.* She realized that her sudden need for fun in her life might be coming with her dealing with her father's mortality and perhaps he was right when he told her not to waste time and to make time to enjoy your life.

The thought, without hesitation, was gruesome and something she really wished not to deal with. That time, hers or his, would eventually come and her level-headed behavior would ultimately take charge. It quickly occurred to her that she had never invited her dad to visit her in Manhattan. Maybe it was out of fear that he would say no, but honestly she just couldn't picture him being comfortable in the big city, Maybe with age came curiosity and he would want to.

The next morning Sara went shopping, which was somehow rewarding in that she was finally doing some-thing for herself. But shopping during the holiday sea-son in New York took enormous patience, not only for the crowds on the sidewalks but also in the stores. Sara had forgotten that during the season the stores hired all sorts of seasonal help and that in itself was a challenge.

Last minute shopping gets you what you deserve, she thought. *I should have planned this much better but doing something impulsive has its own reward.*

Unlocking her door she took her bundles into the bedroom to see what else would be required for the holi-day gathering. Sara removed her new dress from the gar-ment bag. Looking at her choices, she remembered how much she had spent on this little number and the shoes and the jewelry and she fought the urge to return it all immediately.

Her sartorial discovery in the little boutique on Park Avenue was made for seduction and perhaps would make more of a statement that she intended to make. Hanging the dress on the closet door, she stood back and looked at the couture creation. The color was the latest steel blue with thin spaghetti straps, a very deep plunging neckline and clinging flowing sides in floor length. The provocative slit up the side would most certainly show off her long and shapely leg and get the proper attention. *Well, this will undoubtedly wake up some people, assuming I have the nerve to show up in it.*

Reaching into the shopping bag she took out the shoes she had chosen to go with this retro dress fit for a 1950s movie star. The sales lady did call it contemporary, so perhaps that was the right word. She wondered to herself why the hardest part of this day was finding the right shoes. In any case, she managed to settle on a style that she had never worn. Describing her new shoes as high heels was an understatement as they were at least six inches tall. The sling back strapping gave them sleekness and showed off her feet very well. Matching in color to her dress with bright stones on the instep made them sparkle, and more than likely would catch an eye or two. "Yeah, this should do it. I will either be the hit of the party or get busted for street walking."

Trying the dress on in the boutique certainly made it clear that very little in undergarments were going to be needed. This beautiful and stylish work of art did not accommodate a bra, which was a problem, especially with Sara's feminine pulchritude. The sales lady Noreen, a beautiful and well dressed young woman, suggested a particular tape and seemed very happy to show her how to use it. It occurred to her at the time that maybe Noreen was having just a tad too much fun, but she let it go as she was in need of assistance, or perhaps she was in need of some personal attention by someone. Down deep she knew her lack of social life was her fault and with the New Year coming perhaps she would have a resolution or two of her own.

CHAPTER SIX

Dr. Stewart's nurse had called and asked Jon to come to the office to meet with the doctor to discuss his test results. Jon was feeling very mixed emotions about this day as he had concerns about what the test results would reveal but on the positive side, he was very anxious to see Dr. Lovely again. *Damn, she is attractive and after all, why not fantasize, even at my age?*

As he approached the VA hospital he could not help but notice all the men and women coming and going, and for the most part, they were sad. Many seemed almost robotic as if they went through life out of habit. He felt bad, as he knew they were all vets and most were most likely in worse shape than him. Some had injuries from many years past. Some were young, wearing prosthetics, which was the hardest for him to see. He just could not understand what piece of earth anywhere was worth a Marine's life? He also knew that dwelling on that would do no good and that his duty today was to himself and Sara. Perhaps today he would have answers that would point the way to what lay ahead.

He checked in at the desk and was told they would call him to the examining room shortly. Jon sat down and reached for a magazine when a squeaky little voice called his name. When he looked up a young nurse was standing there smiling at him. *Good grief she looks like she is still in high school.* Jon quickly followed the rather energetic nurse into the examining room.

She took his blood pressure, temperature and weighed him, all very efficiently like she had done this a thousand times, probably because she had. When the nurse completed her tasks, she told him Dr. Stewart should be right in and left quickly to get to the next patient. Through the door he could hear her voice squeaking out the name of the next patient, then fading not at all too soon. *Whatever the news is I am ready to deal with it and do what I need to do,* Milo thought to himself.

The door abruptly opened and Dr. Lovely stepped in. She was truly a sight for old, sore eyes. Her bright smile and "Good morning Sgt. Milo. How are you?" was not a question but rather more the voice of an angel. She was a good person and it was obvious. The entire rabble about her good looks left his thoughts. Jon thought instead how unusual it felt to be addressed by his rank from so long ago, but he did appreciate the apparent respect. "I am doing just fine, Doctor Stewart. And you?" Apparently not having any intentions for small talk, the good doctor got down to business without answering.

"Jon, I have your test results, and I have some genuine concerns. As you are aware, your struggle against the effects of Agent Orange has been progressing and by that I mean your kidney function is lessening. There is no soft way to say this, so I need to be very open with you. There are typically five stages of kidney disease and today by all tests you are between three and four. That, coupled with your blood pressure issues and history, means we need to act now to slow down the progress of your kidney failure."

"Okay Doc, that's about what I expected. What do we do? More pills? Injections? What?"

"Jon, there are no pills that can stop this as most of the damage is being done by blood sugar levels that are too high. Diet and exercise are two of the best deterrents to slowing down the disease."

"What kind of time are we talking about here Doc?"

"Jon that is up to you for the most part. We can monitor your improvement or your ability to slow this down by changing your diet and getting proper exercise, but there is no way to cure or stop it completely. Most importantly we need to lower the creatine levels in your blood to slow down the progression, and diet and exercise best do that.

"Secondly, we have your blood pressure issue. The regimen of medication you are currently taking is working, but with your family history, you do have reason to be concerned so again the diet and exercise is the answer. We also want to keep track of your white cells to be sure Agent Orange is not giving you another gift, such as cancer anywhere in your body."

"Damn Doc, you are full of good news. So, what's next?"

"The nurse will have some guides for diet, and I am sure you know how to exercise; all Marines do. You just have to choose to do it."

"Okay, thanks, Doc. I will as best I can. You do know about old dogs and new stuff?" He took a deep breath. "Say Doc, what do you do for fun if I can ask?"

"Sorry Sergeant, but that is classified," she responded with a smile.

As Jon left the VA Clinic, his mind was reeling from the appointment and the diagnosis he got from Dr. Lovely. *Maybe I am just too old to change my life. I know what I like and well, exercise, that is something I could do. Maybe join a gym and meet some hot divorcees or widows. Now that wouldn't be all bad,* he thought, always in pursuit of a bright side.

Being open and honest with Sara would be the real challenge. *I just can't handle the look in her eyes. I don't want her to start worrying about me. She has her own life, but at the same time, she has the right to know as she has told me on multiple occasions. Somehow she just needs to accept that her father is getting old and so far she hasn't been able to do that. I just need to plan the right time and place to be with her because there is much more than this that I need to share. Now I need to find a gym with some good scenery.*

A smile made its way across Jon's face as he well understood his condition and gave thought to the scenery. *I would take up golf, but I recall what someone once said about that sport: Golf is a good walk spoiled.*

CHAPTER SEVEN

It was party time, and as Sara was getting ready, she struggled just a bit with the taping of her cleavage to avoid any wardrobe malfunctions. When she finished and stood before the full-length mirror on the back of her bedroom door, she wasn't sure who this woman was. *Damn, I look good,* she thought. She also chuckled when she realized the mirror was not hers but had been left there, affixed to the back of the door by the previous tenant. *Now that says something about my lack of homemaking.*

In any case, the dress, the shoes and even her makeup was surprising if she did say so herself. She was a bit worried about the side slit in the skirt portion that went to the top of her thigh but the hell with it. *I have beautiful legs,* she thought.

To spoil herself, she made arrangements for a limo to pick her up to and from the party, which was being held at the firm's Chairman's home on the Upper East Side. The weather was pretty cold but at least was dry at the moment. She decided to take a light cashmere pashmina to wrap around her shoulders as she had no plans to be outside and she didn't own a fur coat. She just never felt the need to spoil herself like that. Now if she met a man who wanted to buy her a fur coat, well who knows? She laughed at the thought.

Upon arriving at the party location she was amazed at the size of the home. The entrance alone was more substantial than her living room and bedroom combined. As she exited the limo, she smiled to herself as she felt a bit like a princess heading into the ball. She was equally aware that in reality, it was more like a snake pit, but tonight she would be the snake charmer and handle the snakes. Uppermost in her mind was how to avoid her nemesis Stefan Wood, the prima donna associate, who was always trying to impress everyone. Perhaps he wouldn't even be there, she hoped. As she walked up the immense stairway to the massive entry doors that were opened by a staff member she could hear the holiday music playing.

Of course, as it would happen the first person she would see that she knew was the idiot Stefan Wood. However, as she approached him, she chuckled at how far his jaw dropped and also how evident it was that his eyes went to her cleavage. Noticing his shock she couldn't resist messing with him. She whispered in his ear as she glided by. "Yes Stefan I do have tits, and this is as close as you will get, so close your mouth, stupid."

At first she was somewhat disappointed that no one approached her to say hello but suddenly standing beside her was the boss of the boss, Mrs. Lucille Evans. Lucille was a lady of elegance and certainly had more class than her husband and was surprisingly gentle for a lady of her stature and means. She extended her hand to welcome Sara, and as she took her hand, she genuinely expressed pleasure at having Sara attend. "Sara, so glad you could make it, and by the way you look amazing. It is so nice to have someone here that doesn't look like a lawyer.

"I suspect some of these 'gentlemen' will be tripping all over themselves around you. You have a great time, and maybe we can have a quiet chat a bit later."

She looked at Sara then and continued. "I did hear about your quest on behalf of your Dad, and I think that is a wonderful thing to do. I hope you can make it happen."

"Mrs. Evans, do you mind if I ask how you found out about this?" asked Sara. "About a month ago my husband and I were having dinner with Congressman Platt and the difficulty of making this a reality was shared with us by the Congressman. I hope that is permissible," she answered.

Sara thought to herself so much for confidentiality. "Of course I was just curious. I have been working through the Congressman's office people, and I have been planning to try to have a conversation with him but so far we have never met. "

"Well, pretty lady, would you like to meet him? He is here this evening. In fact, he is standing right there with that group. The Congressman is the tallest and he is very handsome as well. Just remember, he is a politician," she said with a smirk.

"I will meet him later," Sara answered. "He looks a bit tied up, and I want to get my bearings first if you understand."

"Honey I certainly do. Most likely he will find you once he sees you," Mrs. Evans said with a wink.

Sara could only hope she didn't let on to Mrs. Evans the sudden rush of blood to her head and other places as she saw this handsome tall and well, drop dead gorgeous hunk. *Sara, calm down,* she told herself.

She did her best not to stare while she made her way through the crowd to the bar. Reaching the bar she decided to order a Manhattan to start the evening. Maybe she needed some serious liquid courage as she was apparently out of her comfort zone in unfamiliar ways, While Sara waited for the handsome bartender to make her cocktail she stole another glance in the Congressman's direction. Smiling to herself she was happy to see her first impression was reinforced by the second look.

As the evening wore on, she mingled successfully and managed to make small talk with co-workers most of which are men. She had some fun seeing the looks on their faces as they realized who this vision was. They were used to the lady lawyer that wore button-upped blouses, blazers and long skirts, with sensible shoes and minimal makeup every day in the office.

One of her close friends at the office Abigail who was always trying to get her to have more style and use her femininity at work was aghast but with excitement and not jealousy. Abby calmly walked over to her and guided her by the arm away from the crowd and whispered in her ear. "Seriously, you save all of this for a Christmas party? You look hot girl, but I have to ask; what did this getup set you back?"

Sara laughed and answered, "You don't want to know. Really! But thank you."

As their conversation drifted to the apparent politicking going on at this party, Sara felt someone approaching her from behind. She turned slowly and saw the Congressman coming to a stop very close and as he extended his hand he introduced himself. "Good evening Miss Milo, I understand you are one of the top attorneys that work with Mr. Evans. Allow me to introduce myself; I am Devon Platt."

Sara smailed at him, encouraging him to continue. "I should also tell you that Mrs. Evans told me who you are. I just had to meet you to be able to stop staring at you from across the room. Such a lovely, lovely gown and those great shoes, I couldn't help staring." he added.

Oh, my, Sara thought. He *notices things too....* "Thank you, Mr. Platt, and so very lovely to meet you. Are you an attorney as well?" she asked.

"I used to practice law, but now I work for you. I am your congressman, assuming you live in New York," he admitted.

"So you are that Platt! Sara remarked feigning ignorance. "Perhaps you are aware of my contacts with your staff regarding my father."

"So you are that Sara Milo," he responded, also with feigned ignorance. "Yes, I am familiar, and more importantly, I am pushing it up the ladder as quickly and as much as possible so far."

"Well, Congressman what do you think of my chances?" Sara asked.

"There is so much background work involved such as eyewitnesses, testimony and record checks that are perhaps the most difficult. Record keeping during the Viet Nam war was not very good as computers were not available at all back then. Overall I would say the odds are against it happening, at least at the level we want.

But you never know and no one is giving up yet at all." he explained.

"Congressman, I appreciate that."

"Please, call me Devon," he responded. The Congressman, not one to miss an opportunity, looked into her eyes, took her hand and asked, "Would you care to dance?" t

He guided her to the dance floor without waiting for an answer.

Boy, this guy likes to take the lead, Sara thought to herself.

As they approached the dance floor, it was evident that many eyes were on them and Sara's feelings were in turmoil. On the one hand, she had a desire to be swept away by the handsome, articulate intelligent and well-dressed dreamboat. But more importantly, she needed to find a solution to her problem.

She decided just to let things happen and see how far they would go. As they fell into the dance, she felt the Congressman's firm hand on the small of her back just barely above her waist. He gently encased her hand with his other hand. Her body melted into him, and they moved as one to the beat of the slow dance music playing. For Sara, it was like they were the only two in the room and it was all about the chemistry she was feeling. As much as she was enjoying the dance, her cautious self was still on alert.

Neither of them spoke during the dance but a lot of communication was there between them, and perhaps that silent conversation was even more powerful than words.

As the song ended, the Congressman thanked Sara for the dance, offered her his card and invited her to call him any time. Sara had never felt so aroused in such a short time in her life and couldn't help wonder what would happen next, if anything.

The rest of the evening went by quickly, and the party was slowly thinning so she texted her limo that she was ready to go home. As she was leaving, Mrs. Evans caught up with her to say goodbye and thank her for adding such class to her event. "Sara, I know we hardly know each other, but we ladies must look out for each other as much as we can. I want to let you know that Devon Platt is one of the good guys and he is a serious man of integrity so if that is important to you, then do not be afraid."

"Thank you so much for caring, Mrs. Evans. I hope we have time together again soon."

Walking out into the evening, Sara felt she had overcome some demons in not only how she looked but also how she handled herself. It felt good. As much as she would like to have a social life, perhaps even with this new man, she had to stay focused on her dad for now and keep things in perspective. But it had felt great to be the object of attention for a change.

The limo ride home was not long, but it offered the opportunity for reflection, mostly about the events of the evening. Sara decided she enjoyed the party much more than she expected and somewhere in the back of her mind felt a sense of satisfaction at having made clear she was a woman of many facets. She would, however, be glad to get home and undo this tape that had maintained a bit of her sense of dignity and prevented exposing too much of her femininity.

She smiled to herself. *I am so damn proper, even in my thoughts. Need to work on that.* Of course, the most significant surprise had to be meeting the Congressman. The dance was the magic of the evening, and the chemistry she felt was real. And while it was necessary to maintain her poise, she could have easily been more adventurous. She mused to herself; *did he sense what I felt? Time will tell.*

Arriving home, she carefully removed her dress and hung it in her closet, where if a garment could have feelings, it must have felt it was in a foreign country. Feeling very naughty after such an exciting and unusual evening she slid between the sheets without her usual pj's. *All the better to have a pleasant dream,* she thought as she turned out the light.

CHAPTER EIGHT

Jon awoke with a start. He was sweating like crazy even though his bedroom was a bit chilly. Nothing unusual for him; dreams often were the cause and last night was no different. Fortunately, for Jon, his ability to recall the details was rare. Perhaps this failure was for the best, even though it was often frustrating. In years past, mornings like this could arouse anger, sorrow and fear in him and his reactions to those feelings would often frighten Serena, and later on Sara. As the years went by Jon had learned to control his emotions and much of that ability was because of his father's guidance. At this point in his life he had learned that while the nightmares were not going away he would not let them control his life. *Maybe this aging thing does have some advantages.* Before making his way to the kitchen the first order of the day was always to take his prescribed medicine. If he failed to follow the routine, there was a better than even chance he would forget later on. Naturally, the first cup of coffee came next.

As he poured his coffee, he grabbed the TV remote to turn on the news, not that there was much he was interested in hearing or seeing. He did like to keep tabs on any story involving the VA and loss of life in the current war locations. Times were sure different than in his day. Christmas was fast approaching, and it was essential to have a plan as he was so looking forward to Sara coming to spend the holiday with him. This time of year was always full of mixed emotions. He missed his wife Serena every day, but he missed her even more when he and Sara were together. Like most people his age he just could not believe how fast the time had flown. Sara was now a grown woman of accomplishment and beauty with a loving and caring way about her. It was, at times, very difficult looking at her as she looked so much like her mother. *I wonder if she will be expecting me to have a tree here*, he thought. *Well, no matter, I will get one and be sure to have plenty of wood for the fireplace.* He recalled how much women are all about ambiance and feel.

The question consuming his mind was how to share with her his illness and what expectations she should have. He also needed to tell her more about his life and how he became who he was, and more importantly, how he came to make the significant decisions in his life.

As he listened to the TV, it was plain that the focus of the morning was all politics, and politicians spouting off to make themselves sound and look important. *Damn what a waste of time these people indeed are. Enough of this crap, I need to get a tree and get this place ready to show Sara her dad is still living a good life.* He also thought to himself, *okay dummy, where are your gifts for her?*

As he went to get dressed for the day he was thinking about a gift for Sara. He wanted it to be something memorable and lasting. Something that she could hold onto during any troubled times ahead which were part of life. What could he do that would be a way for her to remember the good times and hold on to the priceless memories of her past, which in all essence was her birthright. Then it came to him.

Somewhere in the attic was an old chest full of childhood photos of her and many of them all at various places and gatherings. Could he go through them and put together a memory book for her to keep and one day pass on to her children? *Well that's a nice thought, but when I share it with her I will leave the children part out,* he thought, with a smile. *I don't have a lot of time but I can do this,* he thought, *and perhaps find some lovely bauble that she might wear. My girl doesn't know how beautiful she is and maybe that is part of what makes her so unique. The question remains; how do I tell her all that she needs to know?*

Grabbing his cup of coffee, he made his way up the stairs of his house he'd built back in the eighties. Like most people, he had become accustomed to his surroundings and rarely gave it much thought, but for some reason this morning he noticed details such as the wall color, which at the time was quite popular. He had long forgotten the name of the color but it was about the color of a white egg so probably called something like eggshell white or some lame name but it had worn well as best he could tell.

Since he had not remarried, there seem to be no reason to remodel the house. No doubt the house could use a touch of remodeling, but that would almost certainly require being willing to part with some of the memories the home held for them both.

He believed Sara had an exciting life in New York, but he often wondered if she would have an interest in owning her childhood home somewhere down the road. That would make him happy, and that was the only thing that could kindle any interest in taking on a significant project. It had been a while since he worked and had in the recent past came close to selling all of his tools that he once used every day. When he went to the top of the stairs and looked up at the crawl space ladder that would unfold when he pulled the string he remembered years ago telling Sara that she needed to stay out of the attic as she might encounter some monsters. Trying hard to scare her, she never really bought any of what he had to say on the subject. *No doubt she was always smarter than me,* he thought, grinning.

After climbing up into the attic, he was amazed at how organized it all was. Memories were everywhere. Some of Sara's toys were on display, like the dollhouse he had built for her one Christmas. In one corner stood the rocking chair his wife used every night getting Sara to sleep when she was fighting the infant colds that always seemed to be causing problems for the hardworking family.

Against the far wall he spotted the one trunk he knew the contents of. The label in big letters "USMC" was difficult to miss. He knew it contained his old uniforms and other memorabilia from his days i the Corps. It had been many years since he opened that trunk and saw no reason to do so on this night. *Smiling to himself he thought it would be interesting to see if he could still fit into the dress blues he was so proud of.* However, that was a challenge for another time perhaps. His love for the Corps would always be part of him and that conflict of love of Corps and hatred of war would somehow, some day need to be resolved.

I know there is another trunk up here somewhere. I am sure it contains several photo albums. I can't remember why I would save all of this stuff. I need to clean this place out. After a short search, moving all sorts of junk, the old trunk revealed itself. Dusting off and opening the lid, Jon began to smile as he realized how appropriate his plan was for the occasion. Pictures of their whole life that Sara would barely remember would be put to good use in a book for her Christmas present.

Near the bottom of the trunk, he came across a book he hadn't seen in years. It was his graduation book from Parris Island USMC boot camp. *Damn, I did not know this was still anywhere. It belongs in that trunk over there he thought as he glanced at the trunk across the way.* As he leafed through the pages, it boggled his mind that he was once so young. He also was fully aware that it would not be a good idea to dwell on the past, so he continued on the mission at hand.

As he dug deeper into the trunk, Jon found much of what he had been seeking. Carefully he caressed the cover of the album that his late wife Serena, his so very young bride at the time, had put lovingly together. Jon was a bit apprehensive knowing that inside was going to be a combination of pain and happiness. He also knew that it was time to face both sides of his life, to deal with the painful memories and allow himself to cherish the good ones.

When he opened the album cover, he found in her old school style delicate handwriting, their names as a family. Serena, John and Sara Milo, dated 1976. Sara had just been born. Their life was terrific when he was able to remind himself how lucky he was. It was also a time of struggle for this young Marine who had returned home from his combat tour in "The Nam." ten years earlier.

Jon was not here to focus on that and resisted the urge to go down the dark path. No, he was determined to gather all the right things for a memory book to give to Sara for the fast approaching Christmas holiday. As Jon gathered up many of the photos that Serena had lovingly kept, he came across a handful of photos that were of his Serena's family, and many of her mother's relatives who had never left the old country. Sadly he had never really kept in touch with that side of the family. Serena was Italian and her grandparents, plus no telling how many cousins, still lived in the Naples area of Italy. He doubted that the Nona, as she was named, would still be alive. Sara never had a chance to know her Mother's side of the family except for her grandparents from Boston. Sara knew she was of Italian heritage and was very proud of that side of her family and had often said that she wished she could learn more about her mom's family.

Then the idea hit Jon. Why shouldn't she, and why shouldn't he? *I can make that happen. I can arrange to take Sara to Italy for a couple of weeks. We can spend some real time together, and hopefully, she can discover her heritage and perhaps we can come to know each other better than ever.*

We have always been close, but I have kept her locked out in so many ways, and it is the time that ends. It is going to take some time to find out where we need to go and so forth so I will need to plan this. Her birthday is in May so what a better birthday present.

The only roadblock he could think of would be if she would be willing to take that much time away from the office. That could be a challenge. It was more than worth a try. He put the album under his arm and left the attic. *Damn, I am excited about this,* he said to himself with a smile.

CHAPTER NINE

Sara awoke with a start when the alarm went off and she slowly remembered the events of the previous evening. Stretching her legs and arms, she felt terrific. For the first time in a long time, she felt empowered about taking a chance such as she had done last night. It felt so good to her to have people notice her somewhere besides a courtroom. Feeling she was found to be attractive to men and women gave her a sense of strength. She thought for a moment that perhaps starting in the new year, she would work at being a bit more provocative and less matronly in her appearance and demeanor. Maybe she would not only get more attention, and she could exude a sense of power and authority. She could combine the new her with her obvious legal talents. That could be a deadly combination. *What a possibility,* she laughed. *Why not?*

As she lay there daydreaming, she glanced at the clock and realized she needed to get moving. She was due to pick up her rental car this morning for her drive to her dad's home for the holiday. She was excited. It had been several months since they had been together and she needed more dad time than their twice-weekly telephone calls. She was also hoping to learn more about the past and perhaps feel him out on what his thoughts would be, without telling him about her quest for his very deserved recognition.

Typically she took the train from New York to Boston but for some reason, perhaps her newfound sense of adventure, she wanted to drive. It had been a long time since she had been out of the city and taking a leisurely drive, even with the holiday traffic, would be good for her. Besides that also meant when she was there she wouldn't have to ride around in and borrow her dad's old beater pickup. She did, however, want to observe his ability to drive safely.

As she headed out of the city, the morning traffic was quite heavy but moving well. Fortunately, the weather forecast was promising and would not cause any issue either on the way or the return. Turning on the radio, she found an oldies station that mixed in holiday tunes as well. She loved the oldies that her dad used to listen to when they were in the car together, so it seemed appropriate that she should tune them in for this trip to be with dad for another Christmas.

How she wished her mom was with them, indeed for her but really for her dad. She knew he still missed her very much. To some degree, so many memories of her mom and their times together had somewhat faded, and she found that sad. Maybe she would ask Dad if she could dig around in drawers and places to gather some old photos she could take home with her. She really would like to prevent more memories from fading.

After about an hour and a half of driving Sara decided it was time to take a break and get something to munch on and quench her thirst. When she got out of the car at the roadside diner, she couldn't help but notice some of the stares she was getting. *Okay, so what is this all about?* Sara had decided to dress casually but perhaps a bit more stylish than of late, and it seemed to be having the desired effect. Maybe it was the high-heeled winter boots that showed off the shape of her legs along with her tight jeans. Or perhaps it was the impact of the classic ponytail hairstyle with the bright Christmas red silk blouse that exposed the right amount of cleavage. *What the hell, this is a good feeling. At least people now pay attention. I need to keep it classy though,* she grinned inwardly.

It occurred to Sara that maybe she ought to call Dad and let him know of her expected arrival time. While she was dialing the phone, the memory of the handsome politician popped into her mind. Fortunately when Dad answered she was brought quickly back to reality. "Hi, Dad," Sara said. "How are you??

"Where are you dear one? I'v been worried."

"I'm on my way, and at the moment I am a bit more than halfway. I decided last minute to drive instead of taking the train and you know, it feels good to be in control and able to see more than I could from the train window. So much has changed since the last time I drove this route."

"Okay sweetie, I was wondering about that since I had not heard from you as to when to pick you up at the station," Jon said. He was doing his best not to sound overly concerned.

"I should be there in time for dinner no problem. Can I take you out somewhere, wherever you like?" she asked.

"Honey I have been cooking today just for us so the answer would be no. I have us covered."

"Really? Since when do you like to cook?" she teased.

"I never said I like to. I just said I have, but truthfully I do like to cook for you, just not a lot when it's just me."

"Dad, that explains a lot. Okay, I'll see you soon. By the way, what are we having for this big meal and special occasion?" she asked, just as she heard the click on the other end signaling the end of the conversation.

Well, she thought, *I guess Dad is still short on words.*

About two hours later she arrived at the house. Shutting off the engine she took a moment to take it all in. Through the big picture window, she could see her father chose to put up a Christmas tree, undoubtedly adorned with all the beautiful ornaments from her childhood, each lovingly chosen for particular reasons. For just a brief moment the emotions of her loss so many years ago came flooding back. How she wished her mom was around to see all that she had accomplished.

She thought that this effort by her dad must have been hard on him too after all these years. As she looked around the yard, she could see the remnants of her tree swing in the back, which had never been taken down. The neighboring houses all looked the same and as always right in front of her car in the driveway was the old beater truck Dad loved for some reason.

She thought that with its yellow color and its rust spots it resembled an overripe banana. She wondered if the old truck was even remotely safe for Dad to drive. But knowing him she was reasonably confident that he had maintained it well, merely out of pride and the challenge of keeping it running so he could brag to his friends at the VFW.

Well, I guess I had better go in. If Dad sees me sitting here, he will have too many questions.

As she opened the door, the beautiful spice smells from the kitchen gave her a hint of the roast beef in the oven. The sound of Christmas music came from the living room. Instantly she enjoyed a feeling of home and comfort that she just realized she missed terribly.

"Dad, I'm here. Where are you?" Sara shouted.

Coming quickly around the corner was the bear of a man who she loved with all her heart, and he looked amazing. His shirt had creases, and so did his pants. His hair was well combed, and he even had on a tie.

"Baby girl, I am right here," he said, tossing his apron on a chair and giving her one of his patented hugs that suddenly reduced her to a little girl once more. The embrace seemed to last a long time, and nothing was said nor were words needed. As Sara pulled back from her father's arms, she saw for a brief moment a tear in her dad's eye and realized how much she had missed him as she felt her own eyes filling.

"Dad, it is amazing to see you. I've missed you."

"Same here, Sara Jane. Let us get you settled in your room. You remember where it is?" he questioned with a smirk.

"Okay, okay. Yes, I remember where my room is," Sara shot back. Having dad call her by her first and middle name took her back many years. He was the only one who ever called her that, and she had forgotten how much she loved it.

Jane was her grandmother's name on her father's side, and most likely that was important to him. Once upon a time he only used her initials when he was upset with her; he would speak quite seriously and call her SJ.

Her mother was a great listener and Dad's respect for her mom was something that Sara had learned to appreciate early in life. Sadly, after her mother's passing, the evening meal ritual was less fulfilling, as they both were hurting for a long time. Eventually when Sara went off to college and things naturally changed.

The meal was delicious, and the conversation was somewhat surface for now. Dad asked about her work, and she gave him all the details, leaving out the Christmas party and the elegant and sexy gown as well as the internal feelings she was experiencing. She was pretty sure that would be just a bit too much information for her dad.

The usual small talk was more than pleasant, but in the back of Sara's mind were some serious questions. As usual Sara was anxious for some answers, but also knew that these things would have to happen on his schedule. She never felt comfortable in pushing Dad for answers on sensitive issues. Plus she knew that if she did, he would most likely change the subject as his way of telling her he was not ready to discuss that particular topic.

As they were enjoying their after-dinner coffee, Dad looked like he was trying to make up his mind about something. Just like always she could practically see the wheels turning.

"Dad, What's on your mind? You look like you are miles away," Sara observed.

"Honey, I am so sorry. I didn't mean to ignore you. To be honest, I had a bit of an idea that I am trying to figure out how to share with you."

"Dad, I would say as usual the best way is probably to just come out with it. Whatever it is I promise I will have an open mind." Sara looked at him, waiting.

"Okay, dear one, you are probably right. The other day I was in the attic reminiscing and poking around in all the treasures stored up there, and when I opened an old trunk, I found a collection of old photographs. In amongst our family shots were some pictures your mom got from her mother and her grandparents from the old country. It occurred to me that you might have never had the opportunity to know much about that side of the family. That realization gave me an idea."

He took a deep breath and continued. "How would you like to take a trip with me to Italy to look up your distant cousins and others and learn and get to know your heritage? Most of your Mother's family is from the area surrounding the city of Naples and along the Amalfi coast." Jon reminded Sara.

Dad was smiling like the old days and Sara was stunned, her mouth hanging open, unable to respond.

"Dad, How can we possibly do that? I have work, and you need to be taking care of yourself," she answered.

"Honey, there is no way we can't do this. You certainly need the time off and have earned that right, and my health is fine. My new doctor can give me everything I need to last a couple or three weeks.

"By the way, did I tell you my new Doctor is something?" he asked.

"Dad I am listening. I am sure you have thought this through and probably already have the trip mostly planned. So, tell me more."

"Dear girl, you are right. Here are the basics and we have much more to plan. I am thinking May, as it is an excellent time of year in Italy. We'll fly to Rome and take the new hi-speed train to Naples. Get a driver to take us to Sorrento, and that will be our center of the trip, at least so far. From Sorrento, we can explore the area looking for family and see Capri and the rest of the Amalfi Coast. From the photos I found searching online, it would be a beautiful place to spend some serious quality time with my beautiful daughter. How is that for starters?" Jon asked proudly.

"Dad, you are crazy. Can we really do this? You know it won't be cheap," Sara reminded him.

"Not to worry, I have it covered. This trip will be my treat," Jon beamed. "The only money you will need is for maybe some personal shopping. I hear the Italian fashion world is pretty unique. However, I will need your help in trying to track down your mother's family. That I am not good at yet, but I am sure we can do it."

He continued. "Secretly, it has always been a bucket list trip for me. It is also one I had always wanted to take with your mother, but life got in the way. I also feel it would give us an excellent opportunity to share things that we have kept on the back shelf over the years…and that would be important to me."

Sara thought to herself, *maybe this is what I have been hoping would happen. I need to be patient and let Dad take the lead on this.*

"Okay, Dad, it sounds wonderful, you just let me know what you need from me. By the way, do you have a current passport? And what did you mean your new Dr. is something?" Sara asked.

"I meant she is lovely and not like any of the others at the VA, and no I don't have a passport yet. However, I went to the post office two days ago, filled out the papers and even got my picture taken. They said about six weeks, so I paid the extra for expedited, so I should have it sooner. Does that surprise you?" Jon said with a huge grin.

"Not surprised at all. You have always done whatever you needed to do. I will have to do the same," Sara admitted.

Not long after, while Sara was doing the dishes, dad came around the corner and let her know he was going to bed. He gave her an enormous hug and a kiss on the cheek and the forehead just like he had always done at bedtime.

He told her, "Sleep in as long as you want. I will have the coffee ready, and we'll make breakfast whenever. No rush, it's a holiday!"

As she watched her Dad walk down the hall to his room, she wondered to herself how, after all these years, was he able to still sleep in the same room as he had with her mother for so many years. Maybe he found comfort in that. Then again, perhaps it was because it was all he knew and he had no interest in distancing himself from their life together.

She admired his strength to continue to enjoy his life. She knew he had many friends, played golf, and enjoyed helping neighbors and friends with their projects, all of which kept him busy after he sold his business and had retired.

As she looked around the house, almost nothing had changed. Dad at some point had given the indoors a new coat of paint, but he was a man who liked what he liked and saw no reason to change for change sake. She could also tell that her father still wore his and her favorite cologne, Old Spice, that never seemed to be out of date, sort of his trademark if he had one.

Smiling to herself, she wondered if something was going on with the pretty, new doctor. She doubted that would be the case with ethics and all, but she couldn't help be pleased that Dad had noticed. Maybe he had more going on than he was sharing.

It was about 9:30 and for her a bit early to sleep so she decided to curl up on the couch and relax and try to make sense of her life. She loved her work, but she now could see the need to have other pastimes and people in her life. She had had only one serious relationship several years back and that had ended painfully and indeed was to a high degree the reason she was so closed off from the idea of romance.

With that thought in her mind, she came back around to the Congressman. "Damn, why is he so stuck here," she said out loud as she slapped her forehead. Taking stock, he was indeed handsome and the way he held her when they danced undoubtedly got her juices flowing, but she hardly knew him. No doubt it had to be a purely physical attraction, and she thought that maybe that wasn't all bad.

But then again he was a Congressman, so he had to have strengths and talents. He was, as one might expect, extraordinarily confident and she did like that a lot. Well, whatever the attraction it wasn't going anywhere very soon. Perhaps after the holidays they would meet again. Truthfully, she knew they would, as she wanted answers to what she wanted for her father. Giggling, she thought, *what would I do if he were wearing Old Spice? Would that be good or bad?*

Christmas this year was on Saturday, so she had the whole weekend to spend with Dad. She would have to head home Sunday afternoon, probably after church if she knew her father. It would be nice to go to church with him, and she knew he would want her to meet his friends and most likely the minister, since she had no idea who that was.

The best part of walking beside my gentle bear of a father is the feeling of pride and the enormous love I feel for him. The Christmas music will be beautiful.

Sara woke at her usual time at 6 a.m. At first she was upset that she woke up so early on a holiday. Then she remembered it was Christmas morning and not a time to sleep in. Dad would be up, and she wanted to spend the early hour with him having their coffee together.

Walking down the stairs in her slippers and PJ's she could hear the fire crackling like it did every year when she was little. She remembered yelling at her father that the fireplace would keep Santa away but Dad handled the explanation well enough to satisfy her. Try as she might she could not remember when she became aware of the truth.

"Good Morning Dad," Sara said as she walked up and threw her arms around him from behind.

"Good morning Sara Jane, did you sleep well?"

"Not bad at all considering," Sara remarked.

"Considering what?" Dad asked, whipping around with a puzzled look.

"Considering the bed is as old as I am, that's what," she said teasingly.

"Oh that, well I don't get a lot of company. Besides, it is your bed and I don't want to get rid of it."

"Dad it is really okay, don't bother," Sara assured him. "By the way, Merry Christmas!"

"Merry Christmas to you too, dear girl." Jon said, beaming as he moved in for a second hug that lasted much longer. It had been a couple of years since they had spent Christmas together. It felt comforting to them both.

"Dad, I have a gift for you so let us get our coffee and open it," Sara suggested.

"Honey, I also have a gift for you in addition to our trip to Italy." Jon went over to the tree and from under it he pulled a box with a huge red bow in the center. The gift-wrap was full of small snowmen and snow angels, very appropriate for a dad who longed for the past with his little girl.

Sara had to go first, so as she recognized the old Christmas paper from years ago a smile came over her face that warmed his heart. Opening the box she pulled out the photo album Dad had put together with the photos he found in the attic. Seeing what was on the inside Sara could no longer hold back her caged up emotions. She slid next to Jon on the couch and held on so tight while she sobbed, seemingly letting out feelings that had been bottled up for some time.

When she was able to collect her emotions, Sara asked him how he knew what she had wanted for so long.

"Honey, I did not know. Something told me it might be important to you, so it was important to me. I am pleased you are happy," he said.

"Okay, it's your turn," she told Jon. "Here is what I decided would be best for the man who has all that he is willing to have." Sara handed him the envelope with the bow taped to the front.

Jon took the envelope and gave his Sara a look that was a combination of curiosity and fearfulness. He thought to himself, *what on earth could she put in this that would be for me?*

As he felt the surface of the envelope for a clue, he wondered what she was up to this time. Opening the envelope slowly and looking up at Sara for a hint from her expression he finally tore open the inner envelope, and as he began to read, a smile came over his lips. She had bought him a membership to the health club not far from the house. In fact, it was the same club he had thought about joining himself but just had not taken the time to make it happen.

"Okay you, what is this all about? Is this your way of saying I am out of shape or something?" he laughed.

"Dad, not at all. But it is my way of saying you need to take better care of yourself because I want you to stay around for a long time. Besides, I thought maybe you could meet some people and make some new friends at the same time," Sara suggested.

Smiling broadly, Jon reached out and put his arm around his fantastic daughter. "Honey, it just so happens that beautiful new doctor told me to get more exercise and I was planning on doing just that, so now I have to, thanks to you," he responded.

The hug lasted a long time as each enjoyed the particular holiday moment and Jon found himself needing to turn away quickly as the tears filled his eyes and he did not want Sara to see them.

"Merry Christmas, dear one. I love you," he said as he moved away.

As a way to hide his emotions of the moment, he stepped across the room to the fireplace to tend to the fire even though it was burning just fine. He thought to himself, *I need a minute to get control here.*

Sara watched as Jon poked at the fire and she could tell it was an unnecessary gesture, but she would not embarrass him by questioning his actions. Surveying the living room Sara noticed the family photos from years past still in the same places they had always had been. The room had warmth to it that never failed to make her feel comfortable.

She looked to the mantle where she hung her stockings as a young girl, the hearth where she would often sit and stare into the fire which made her feel secure, and even the bookshelves that held so many books of all sorts that were treasured by her mother so long ago. Her dad had changed almost nothing in all these years, which pointed to his holding on to the past with a grip he refused to loosen.

"Dad, can I ask you what your favorite holiday memory is?" Sara asked.

Jon turned to look at her and asked, "Do you mean Christmas or all holidays and how far back can I go? My childhood or adulthood?"

"Well dad, I think I mean since I have been around," Sara said.

"Well, of course, there were many with mom and you and then so many with just she and I, but if I had to pick one, in particular, it would have been one Christmas Eve, the year after your mom left us. I doubt that you would remember, but you and I went to church. When we left the church it was snowing heavily, but so quietly, and at that moment as we walked hand in hand through the snow I was sure I could feel your mother's presence beside us. It felt like she was telling me everything was going to be all right.

"I remember you looking up at me with your big brown eyes and holding my hand so tight that words were unnecessary. We walked in silence and listened to the soft breeze in the air and the snow falling so gently. It was like we were the only three people in the world. That night will be with me forever for many reasons."

As Sara listened to her dad's memory sharing, she was in shock. He had described almost perfectly what she thought was her dream. Now she knew it was not a dream, but a memory that somehow she had held onto without realizing. "Dad, I have a dream almost identical except I am coming out of a church in the city. All very strange."

The rest of the day was spent looking at the photos Jon had collected, and they shared their memories of the days of old. Sara reflected during the day that this was some of the best time she had spent with him in several years. She made a promise to herself this day that for the foreseeable future her relationship with her father would be the most essential part of her life as long as he was with her.

The next morning, as she was getting ready for church, Dad knocked on her bedroom door. Opening the door, Sara found her dad standing there in his best suit and on his jacket lapel was a ribbon, worn by Marines on their uniforms. Sara recognized it as his Viet Nam Service Ribbon with the yellow, green and red colors. She thought it a bit curious why he would have it on his jacket going to church but decided against asking him his reasons.

"Good Morning sweetie, Are you about ready for church?"

"Good Morning Dad. Yes, I am if you are. Is it ok with you if I drive?" Sara asked.

" Sure I have nothing against riding in a new car and besides, I wouldn't want you embarrassed getting out of my old beater at the church," he teased her.

"Dad, That isn't true at all. I just want to chauffeur you today," Sara insisted.

"If you say so. By the way, I always visit your mom after church if you want to go with me."

"Dad, that would be wonderful. I was planning a visit myself, so going with you is perfect," Sara added.

This is not going to be easy for either of us, Sara thought to herself. *We haven't done this together for a very long time.*

Arriving at the church, Sara parked the car and on the way up the sidewalk she took her dad's arm and held on tight. He returned the gesture as he covered her hand with his and it seemed to Sara that this was a huge part of her life she had been missing. Not so much the church part as the closeness of the man she most admired all of her life.

She couldn't help notice that so many people acknowledged her dad on the way in, and more than one lady gave him a solid once over. She had often wondered why Dad had never sought another relationship and that worried her. Her mother had passed away more than twenty-five years ago, and yet Dad never moved on. She was very sure her mom would have wanted him to. Maybe one day he would share that with me as well as so many other things.

The church service was pleasant enough, and the old hymns she grew up with warmed her heart and created the mixed emotions she expected. As they were leaving the church, she noticed an old friend of hers standing at the end of the sidewalk near the parking lot. As she approached, the man in her sight looked at her and smiled and reached out to shake her hand.

"Sara, it is you?" said Jeremy. "I thought it was when I saw you in church and I wasn't sure. You look so different. Are you just visiting or are you coming back home to stay?"

Jeremy was a short-term high school boyfriend that Sara was crazy about for a while in her sophomore year. He was the best athlete in the school and was also on the debate team. However, he was never satisfied with one girlfriend, so Sara had dumped him when she discovered his penchant for multiple women.

"Hi Jeremy, how are you? I just came home for the holidays to spend time with Dad and get out of the city for a while," Sara explained.

"I heard that you were a high powered lawyer in the big city these days and I can only imagine you are doing very well. Good for you. How long will you be staying in town?" Jeremy asked, obviously giving her a significant evaluation.

"I leave this afternoon to drive back right after Dad and I visit the cemetery. What are you doing these days?" Sara asked, being polite though she didn't care much what he was up to.

"Well, I'm the phys ed teacher at the high school. I also coach the football and baseball teams," Jeremy boasted.

"That's great, Jeremy. It was good to see you. Take care. I need to run," Sara said, hurrying to catch up with her father.

As she joined her dad on the way to the car he asked, "Is that the same knucklehead you went out with back in high school?"

Trying not to laugh Sara said, "Yes dad, it is."

"Well honey, I would say you dodged a bullet there," he said with a smile.

"That is true," Sara agreed. "So true."

Arriving at the cemetery they discovered the roads into the lots were not plowed and Dad teased Sara, "If we brought my truck it wouldn't be a problem."

"Dad, this is a rental car with front wheel drive, so it is still not a problem." She gunned the engine to break through the initial snowbank. Fortunately, it was not deep.

Making their way to her mother's plot, Sara looked around and saw the cemetery with older eyes and the perception was very different. For the first time, she got the feeling that it was a place of peace and reverence and not just a cold place with lots of stones with names. Of course at this time of year there were no leaves on the trees and the roads were snow covered. Only a few tire tracks from other visitors were evident.

While they walked from the road to the gravesite Sara reflected back to the day they buried her mother. At the time she was sure it would be the saddest day of her life and until now it was. Even with all the friends and family that attended she recalled feeling so very alone. Alone except for the monumental presence of her Dad and his ability to let her know he was there for her. He was the reason and the light at the end of the tunnel of her despair that allowed her to go on. She would never forget him for that and she new as the years went by one way or another she would always be there for him when he needed her, and now she was sure that time was close at hand.

Mother's monument had her name and dates engraved in the stone like so many others but also had an inscription put there by her dad. The simple but perfect epitaph read: "Serena Milo, Wife, Mother, Friend and Angel." At the top of the stone was a carved angel, representing what she had meant to them both. Sara wiped her eyes and grabbed her father's hand. As they each said their silent prayers they shared a moment that was from the past but yet was so much a part of the present.

Jon gently and quietly reached into his pocket for his handkerchief, which Sara remembered he always had with him for such occasions. First, he handed it to her and then he wiped his own eyes. Neither of them needed words. The silence was appropriate. Finally, Dad took her hand and led her away right after he placed a gentle kiss on the wings of the angel and dusted the fallen snow from the headstone.

Sara was sure that this was a scene her Dad had repeated over the years. She knew he had been there as the stone was spotless unlike many others around her. Most of the monuments were forgotten or neglected by the families and by the custodians of the cemetery as well.

When they arrived at the house, Dad went into the kitchen to make some coffee and Sara went to her room to pack. When she finished packing, she went into the living room and sat next to Jon.

The holiday was over, and it was time to drive back to the city. As she prepared to load the car, she wanted one last look around the home where she had spent her happy childhood. Fearful that something was going to change, Sara went into the kitchen and recalled her Mother cooking her breakfast and so many excellent meals.

She could almost smell the baking cookies and frying bacon. Standing in front of the sink Sara had a view of the backyard, and there was the swing she had spent so much time on, hanging by a single frayed rope. It was sad for Sara to see to that special memory in such condition. It was obvious that Dad did not have the heart to take it down. His pattern for never changing anything was undoubtedly a common theme here, and Sara knew that was okay; it seemed to give him comfort.

Dad was waiting for her outside near the car and had cleaned her windows all around. As she loaded her luggage into the trunk, she knew he was close by, and she could sense a foreboding of saying goodbye. Turning, Sara reached for her dad, and once again they were in a bear hug embrace. She decided against saying much so as not to force him to respond. Merely the big hug, a big smile and a touch of the cheek were his words well beyond any vocabulary.

As Sara started the car, she glanced back at the man who had been the most significant influence on her life and the one constant who was always there whenever she had needed him. A sincere wave and a last smile were all that were required. In a few months, they would be off on their adventure to the old country.

Sara arrived home just a bit later than she expected due to the holiday traffic and some areas of rain along the way. Not really in any hurry she had driven carefully, not focusing on the time it was taking. Walking into her apartment felt strange after the time back home and the stark reality of how barren and cold her apartment was. She vowed to take the time to make her place better for herself. At the same time, she wondered how long she would be here and if it made any sense to do too much.

Spreading out the mail she had collected from her box, she spotted a letter with a Congressional return address. She stared at the envelope for a moment, wondering if she wanted to know what was inside. It had been a great long weekend, and she did not need any disappointments now. Nevertheless, she needed to understand the contents. She read. Headquarters Marine Corps had completed its background investigation into the combat incident in question. The request was moving to the next level for consideration. It was signed by Congressman Devon Pratt with a hand written note to please call him.

Well, that would appear to be good news. The medal request was not declined so far. As Sara recalled the night of the Christmas party, she couldn't help wonder if the Congressman wanted her to call him for professional reasons or personal. Smiling to herself, she said out loud, "Does it matter?"

Yes of course it mattered. What made this man so fascinating to her? Was he perhaps just a touch too polished? She really needed to do some homework here before she got too far into this.

CHAPTER TEN

Jon sat in his favorite recliner chair in his living room staring out the picture window and watching the softly falling snow. He thought the old chair should be retired, but it was still so comfortable even if it was ugly and worn. *I have enjoyed many great naps in this chair, and like many other things in my life, old does not make them useless.*

It did not look like the snowfall would be lasting very long as no significant storms were forecast. A young boy across the street was doing his best to gather enough snow to begin building a snowman. Smiling to himself, John said out loud, "Young man, you have a lot of tenacity and perhaps one day you will be a Marine. Just maybe by the time you are old enough the world won't need Marines." *Fat chance* he thought, but it was a nice dream.

Sitting there he could hear the fire crackling behind him, and his thoughts turned to Sara. Saturday and Sunday had been a wonderful Christmas with his best girl, but there was also some part of him that was sad as he once again missed his bride so much and all the wonderful times they had had at Christmas and all year long.

He couldn't help notice how much Sara reminded him of Serena with her natural beauty, but he also saw she had his posture and carriage in the way she walked, sat and generally moved. It was almost if she had been through Marine Corps boot camp. Chuckling, he realized in some ways she had, and that made him proud. He also came to an understanding this year that memories, with time, became friendlier and less painful and that was a gift to be sure.

Jon thought to himself that now in his retirement he had much more time to reflect and recall parts of his life. He thought more and more often about Viet Nam and wondered to himself if others were doing the same. He realized that free time might not be a good thing for him or others. Back when he was working the dreams were intermittent for sure and thoughts would occasionally come back, but for the most part life kept him busy and he focused on his family and work. Today that was all changed. Jon had lots of time to look for answers he might never find.

Keeping busy was the obvious answer and he did need to begin the planning of their trip to Italy right away. The possibilities were endless, and these indeed could be the memories that Sara would hold on to for her future. The importance of that one thought gave him the chills as he realized the responsibility for the task ahead. It wasn't about where they went or what they did, but that they embarked on the adventure together, forging a real connection. That should not be difficult at all as there was never anything between them that was less than wonderful, well except when she was first a teenager. He laughed at the recollection.

Jon fired up the small computer Sara had brought him last year. He didn't like using it and he knew only enough to be dangerous. As he'd started his search for travel to Italy, he quickly realized that this was a task far beyond his skills. Finding great photos like he had when he'd decided on the trip was one thing. Making a solid plan was another. One quick look revealed hundreds of thousands of articles, websites, and publications dedicated to traveling in Italy. At this rate, their trip might get organized by the time Sara was ready to retire.

Perhaps I should make a list of what we want to do and see and find a travel expert to help us plan. I did tell Sara I would take care of it so I should probably keep my plan to myself.

Reaching for the old faithful yellow pages he began looking through the travel agent listings. He saw an independent agent, a woman with the first name of Brie, and she was not very far from him. The name caught his attention; it had been his other choice for a name for Sara when she was born but the coin flip between he and Serena went to Sara Jane. *I don't remember ever telling Sara how she got her name he mused. Maybe I should share that story soon.*

Dialing the number to speak with the travel agent he wondered if this would work for him. The phone rang and was quickly answered. "Good afternoon, thank you for calling Boston Commons Travel, Brie speaking."

Jon was taken aback at how sweet and lilting her voice was and perhaps even reminiscent of someone he had heard in the past.

"Good Afternoon, my name is Jon Milo. I saw your listing in the yellow pages, and I need some help in planning a trip to Italy for my daughter and myself. Is that something you do?"

"Good afternoon Jon, So glad you called and you really still have the yellow pages?" Brie said, almost choking. "To answer your question, yes I love Italy and have been multiple times myself. I would like to help you put together a fantastic trip for you both. Would you prefer to come to my office or provide some details on the phone now?"

"Well it is a bit complicated," Jon said. "So, yes, if you have the time, I would prefer to meet with you in person to get started."

"Jon, That's fine. How is tomorrow morning about 10 a.m.? Are you available then?"

"Yes, I can make it. I will put together a list of what our thoughts are and bring it with me." "If that will help," Jon said.

"That is perfect Jon, so I will see you at 10 tomorrow."

Could it be she looks as good as she sounds? Nah, no way, he laughed to himself. *Besides, what would you do if she did?*

With one task accomplished, Jon realized it was time to get the house back in order. He'd take down the Christmas tree, put all the decorations away and put Christmas behind him for another year. He remembered that Serena always kept the Christmas season going until New Years and he never could understand that but it seemed necessary to her, so he never asked to change anything. Damn, he loved that woman.

Christmas memories had always been good memories except for one, the Christmas of 1965. Sitting in a foxhole on hill 327 in South Viet Nam he could remember the feeling of loneliness as he stared up at the moon and did his best to stay awake. He recalled the mood of his squad and how much they all wanted to be home, all except one guy on the team. Nathan, a young Marine PFC assigned as Jon's radioman, was from the Deep South in Alabama and his Christmas memories with family were almost nonexistent. Partly because of poverty and partly because of family dynamics, Nathan grew up with little love.

No presents were around on Christmas morning for Nathan and even the Christmas meal was sparse. Hearing Nathan tell about his family was heartbreaking, but this young man was determined to have a better life for himself, which is why he joined the Corps. Jon recalled thinking to himself that he would do his best to be sure Nathan got home in one piece.

Rising from his old chair, Jon thought to himself, *enough with the past and time to get today started.* One last look across the street he saw the young boy was now throwing snowballs at the cars as they passed his point of aim. *That young man had better be careful,* Jon thought, smiling to himself. *If his father sees him, he will be in big trouble, and I know this from experience.*

CHAPTER ELEVEN

Sara awoke to the irritating sound of her alarm, but on this morning she was not unhappy to be getting up. She had a lot to do today after the holiday and foremost in her mind was reaching out to the Congressman about her Dad's medal, and perhaps in the back of her mind, there were more reasons to contact Congressman Platt. *What do I do if he wants to meet in person? More importantly, what do I wear?*

While Sara took some time to spoil herself with a homemade cappuccino, doubts about the Congressman began to creep into her mind. On the surface he seems like a good man but there was something about him that had her concerned. Sara had a lot of experience with devious men in business and in law and somewhere in the back of her mind her spidey senses were on alert.

He just seemed to good to be true. He was very polished and practiced and in Sara's experience that was never good. He also seemed to know exactly how to get through to her; that in itself was a good reason to doubt. Perhaps she needed to do a deep background on the handsome politician and look where she hadn't looked before.

Getting into the shower, Sara passed in front of the mirror and for the first time in a long time she took notice of her body. As she examined herself, she was pleased to see that in spite of her indifference to work-out regimens and healthy eating she had maintained her weight and shape. Sara thought, *pretty damn good if I do say so myself must be in the genes.*

A New Year's resolution popped into her head that she would make time to take better care of herself by adhering to a schedule for the gym and just as fast as it came, it went, fully knowing her work schedule did not allow for such extravagances. *Silly girl,* she thought. Then her thoughts turned to her dad. The holiday had been quite enjoyable, but she sensed something was bothering him and she was concerned that he was holding something back. She also knew that pressing him on anything would close a door. He would deal with whatever it was in his own time and his own way. She believed that she had to trust him to reach out when he needed her.

The surprise of the holiday was the trip to Italy for them both. She wasn't sure what to make of that except he seemed to be interested in spending a significant amount of time with her, which she had wanted for quite some time. Perhaps after all these years, she would finally come to some understanding of what her dad was all about.

If it were possible, she would hope that the medal ceremony could happen before they went off on their trip. Perhaps she'd know more soon.

As Sara left the building, she decided to walk some of the distance as she was undoubtedly early enough. At times she enjoyed the sights and sounds of the city. The cacophony of noise from the traffic, especially the impatient honking of horns that New Yorkers were famous for was almost humorous. Each step of the way provided aromas from the restaurants with coffee and bacon smells emanating from the exhaust fans of dozens of kitchens.

The street Sara lived on housed a long row of brownstones that were well maintained and quite regal. The sidewalks were clean, and even the gutters were free of debris and human discards. Not all the city was anywhere close to the same condition, but for Sara, it was an ideal place. It was mornings like these she could take in the busy world around her and appreciate what her hard work had achieved. The brownstone apartment was expensive and did require a disproportionate amount of her income, but it was so worth it.

After walking about a dozen blocks, she hailed a cab to get to the office. No doubt after a long weekend she had a full plate this morning. Happily, she was confident Victoria would have everything under control. Sara reminded herself to ask Vickie about her holiday.

Riding along the pothole-filled streets in New York was in itself an adventure and a part of the way of life for city dwellers. Cabbies were about as diverse in culture and background as anyone might imagine. This morning it was the silent type, which was okay by Sara. As she watched him maneuvering the crowded streets with well-practiced precision, somehow avoiding multiple collisions of various severities she thought, only in New York.

The photo on the back of the seat showed him to be a young man of most likely middle eastern descent and on the front seat were textbooks that indicated his interest in education, so apparently, he was not planning to be a cabbie long term. She also noticed how clean his cab was, which indeed pointed to his work ethic and sense of responsibility. *Good for him,* she thought.

Just then he pulled to the curb, and as Sara got out, she overpaid him with a generous tip for use in his educational endeavors and said "thank you" and was rewarded by a "Your welcome and thank you," with a smile.

As Sara entered the law offices, she sensed something was amiss. It was unusually quiet for this time in the morning, and particularly for a long weekend, more action should be happening. The usual chatter in the hallways and activity in the conference rooms along the way to her office was missing. When she approached her office, Victoria was nowhere in sight. She began to be worried that something was not right.

Just as Sara was hanging up her coat, Victoria came into her office with a disconcerting look on her face. " Victoria, what is going on here? Where is everyone?"

Victoria responded, "We have a tragedy on our hands. Mr. and Mrs. Evans were on their way back to the city from Connecticut last evening and were in a car accident."

"Oh my God," Sara stammered. "Are they okay?"

"No, Sara, I am sorry, Mr. Evans died from injuries, and Mrs. Evans is in intensive care at the hospital."

"Oh, My God," she said again. "This is unbelievable. Now what?"

"The senior partners have called a meeting for 11:00 am this morning. They have asked that you attend."

" Of course," Sara responded. "Any details available?"

" Not yet," Victoria said. "Certainly nothing about the accident or the meeting."

As Victoria was leaving the office, Sara reminded her to cancel all of her meetings until more was known.

"Of course, I already have done that," said Victoria. "Let me know if you need anything."

Sara sat down, still in shock. Mr. Evans was senior partner and primarily responsible for her growth and ascent up the ranks in the firm. Her boss was a brilliant jurist, and a real gentleman, admired by all who knew him and for a man of such stature was perhaps the most accessible man to approach and talk too.

As the tears began to flow she stared out the window and began to wonder how the company would handle this. It must go on with so many people depending on the firm for their lives and how would their clients respond. Would they be able to continue with the same reputation, not having their founder and senior partner?

Looking out the window, Sara could see the activity far below making her painfully aware that life went on, no matter the circumstances. None of the hundreds of thousands of people scurrying to work or elsewhere had any knowledge that a good man died tragically last night, nor did it change one thing they were planning to do today. This tragedy would be the first personal loss for Sara in her adult life. It occurred to her how lucky she was to still have her dad in her life.

Sara reminded herself that Mr. Evans was such a responsible man that he must have had a succession plan in place so that the firm could go on. After all, it was his legacy and his life, this firm, this family of lawyers and staff. She was confident that the second senior partner Mr. Mason was also a good man who was close to Mr. Evans and would have the best interest of the firm as his compass for the decisions that he would have to make in the coming days.

It occurred to Sara for a moment that her concern for the firm was a bit selfish considering the tragedy, but as a lawyer, it was her job to see the big picture and take on any responsibility necessary for the good of all.

The coming days were going to be at best very sad and uncertain, and the sooner the uncertainty could be eliminated the better for all. What Sara knew without a doubt was Mr. Evans was going to be missed by so many, especially her.

Getting back to the moment she remembered she was supposed to call the Congressman, but knowing that he was friends with the Evans's, the Congressman most likely knew about the tragedy by now. Was a call regarding her interests appropriate? She decided to wait to see how the day went and what she would be asked to do, if anything.

At 11:00 Sara went to the main conference room and found a seat along the wall. The chairs at the conference table were designated only for the name partners and the senior partners. Anyone else in attendance at these formal meeting knew enough to take any seat available somewhere around the perimeter of the room.

Mr. Mason, the senior and name partner who had been with the firm for more than twenty years, called the meeting to order. Sara was a bit surprised that this was going to be a formal meeting and not just a discussion. After making the appropriate remarks about their loss and tragedy he informed those in attendance that instructions left by Mr. Evans in the event of his death were to be read and acted upon as soon as possible. "Based on those instructions," he said, "the following documents are to be opened. They, of course, contain his will, which concerns mostly his family but specific provisions also pertain to the firm.

"With regards to the firm, Our by-laws require a new managing partner to be elected by the name and senior partners as soon as practical, with Mr. Evans' replacement as a name partner to be effective immediately. Taking the appropriate actions is the purpose of this meeting. I will now read a document as written by our late partner Mr. Jeremiah Evans."

Suddenly Sara realized that she was the only junior partner in the room. As her heart skipped a beat, she wondered almost out loud why. What could she have possibly done to be singled out for whatever was coming?

Mr. Mason began. "To my fellow partners, if you are reading this, it means I have moved on, and there are many details which need your commitment and attention. It is also my hope that my wife of so many years

Lucille is well and going on with her life. She and the firm have been my life and love for all of these years, and of course, I have grave concerns about continued growth and prosperity. It is with this in mind that I wish you to accept my choice for my replacement as a name partner, assuming she will agree."

Sara heard the words and realized she was the only other woman in the room. She almost fainted. *This can't be happening. I can't possibly replace this great man. What do I do?*

"Therefore I name Ms. Sara Milo as my successor in this firm. I have all the confidence necessary in her abilities and dedication to make this choice. I trust that all of my colleagues will accept her and support her in the challenges she faces with this change in her life. If for some reason she should decline then I leave it up to my fellow partners to name my replacement."

As Sara stood shaking, the room filled with applause, accompanied by shocked looks on some of the faces. It was at this moment that Mr. Mason walked over to Sara extended his hand. "Miss Milo, do you accept?"

Sara was close to running out of the room but managed to extend her hand and with a firm voice spoke, "I do accept, humbly."

Now that the formality was over the place began to empty. There would be time later for congratulations but for now, the grieving would happen, and the necessary details would have to wait.

Sara began to realize what a huge impact this would have on her life. Prestige yes, money, yes but responsibility was the subject in the forefront. How would she ever follow in this man's footsteps? How could she possibly measure up and be as strong a jurist and have the creative mind he had. *I can't, that is all, I just can't,* she thought.

As she was about to leave the room, she realized she was alone with Mr. Mason, who most likely would be elected managing partner. He approached Sara with an envelope in his hand. "This envelope is to be read by only you in the event you accepted Jeremiah's request."

"Thank you," Sara said, as she started down the hall to her office, unsure of what else to say.

Victoria followed Sara into her office with tears in her eyes and asked, "With this monster change do I get to stay with you?"

Sara reached out and took her into her arms. "Yes of course you do, please don't worry. We can talk a bit later. Right now I have something I need to do alone."

Sara waited for Victoria to leave, then sat and started at the envelope in her hand, almost afraid to open it. It was her boss and mentor speaking to her from the grave. What a morbid thought. Name partner. She'd skipped right past senior partner. How was that even possible? She suspected the answer was in the envelope.

Dear Sara,

This letter is intended to help you understand my decision and to move forward as I know you can. You have the ability and skills of a lawyer far senior in years of experience. Your tenacity and attention to detail are what the firm needs for the future. More importantly, your humanity is the difference between you and other equally skilled lawyers and that is what I hope you will always use to make the tough decisions.

Your love of the law and your concern for people will make the best combination of leadership in my beloved firm. Do not be afraid. Trust your instincts and your abilities and all will be fine. You will no doubt have some challenges. Feel free to gather the opinions of others you trust, but in the end, it is you and your innate goodness you must believe in.

I have enjoyed so much watching your growth and guiding you these years, and I am proud of how you have more than held your own in the competitive environment we chose.

Trust yourself and be happy. As you now know, life is uncertain. Be sure to grab all the wonder of life every day and cherish those you love equally.

Besides, adding the name Milo is only four letters, so not hard to change the sign on the door. Good luck with your pursuit of recognition for your Dad. From all you've told me, he deserves it.

Always your friend and benefactor,
Jeremiah Evans, ESQ

Folding the letter, Sara began to cry uncontrollably. *Better to get it out now and in private,* she thought. And after what seemed like an eternity she got her emotions under control and decided to call her father.

"Good morning Dad, What are you up to?"

"Hi sweetie, Not a lot. Just putting away the Christmas decorations and having a cup of coffee. I am also spying on this little kid across the street while he throws snowballs at passing cars. I suspect he is about to get into some trouble, and it sure is fun to watch. He has a pretty good arm for baseball or throwing grenades even. Maybe a future Marine? Why, what's going on in the big city?"

"Dad we have had some horrible news here," Sara said, and paused, unwilling to say the next part out loud. Finally, "Our managing partner Mr. Evans and his wife were in a bad car accident last night on their way home. Mr. Evans died, and Mrs. Evans is in intensive care."

"Jesus Christ. That's terrible. That has to be a major nightmare for everyone," Jon said.

"It is. It has everyone in turmoil and calling friends and family that they may not have spoken too recently."

So what does it all mean for you?"

"Well, as one would expect from a man like Mr. Evans he did have a succession plan. His documents directed that I be appointed a senior name partner to take his place in the firm."

"That means your name goes on the door?" Jon asked.

"Yes it does Dad, and frankly I am overwhelmed. I never expected this to happen under any conditions, much less such tragic ones."

"Well, honey I am sure the man had a good reason. It is clear he recognized your worth to the firm. I am so proud of you for so many reasons." Jon said. "I know it doesn't feel celebratory at the moment, but congratulations."

"Thank you, Dad. I have much to do, but I wanted to let you know. I don't have any clue at this time if this will change our plans for Italy. I'll do my best not to let it if at all possible."

"Honey, do not worry about me. Do what you need to do and keep me in the loop if you can. I love you so much," Jon replied.

"Thank you, Dad, and I'll talk with you soon. I love you, too."

CHAPTER TWELVE

Tuesday morning came, and as usual, Jon was up early and getting dressed just like he always had. The habits developed in the Corps never left a Marine. He was already starting to think about his appointment with his mysterious sounding travel agent this morning and wishing the time would come sooner.

At about 9:45 Jon arrived at the address he had and walked in the door. The office walls show posters from all over the world along with advertisements on the wall carefully designed to get people to travel to their dream destinations. Looking around Jon could see three ladies at desks on the phone talking very animatedly. Each was staring at the computer screen in front of them, and all seemed very capable from what he could surmise.

As Jon stood by the front counter, a young woman approached him and asked if she could help.

"Yes, I have an appointment with Brie at 10:00."

The young woman smiled and pointed to a corner office. "That's Brie. She should be with you in a moment."

"Thank you." Jon said as he took a seat near the entrance. Looking past the counter, he could watch the woman named Brie, and he thought her quite lovely. In fact, she was elegant. Her hair was perfect and pure white. Her makeup was tasteful and well done in just the right amount, and her clothing looked stylish and colorful. *Now I wish I was better dressed,* Jon thought. *Do not get ahead of yourself. No way is this classy lady going to be interested in an old Jarhead like you.*

Jon looked around at all the oversized travel posters framed on the walls. His mind turned to this idea of a trip to Italy with Sara. *All these years and I have never had any interest in travel. Why is that? It's a big world with so much to see and discover. Why haven't I?*

He knew the answer; he had no interest in going alone and sadly no interest in other women since his beloved Serena was lost. *If Serena could speak to me, I know she would give me some hell for wasting years and not living more fully. I retired well, so no excuse for sure, perhaps this will be the start of something new. It would be appropriate to go on a trip first with Sara. I have so much to tell her and share with her.*

He snapped out of his daydream when he heard her voice. "Mr. Milo. Good morning! I am Brie; we spoke yesterday," she said as she offered her hand.

"Good morning, Yes, we did. I have a list for you." Jon said nervously. *Ok, now I am acting like a high school knucklehead.*

"Excellent," Brie said. "Let's take a look. "

After a moment of reading, Brie smiled and said, "You have a very ambitious itinerary in mind. Are you open to discussion?"

Jon stammered like a kid. "You're the expert, you tell me what makes sense and will accomplish our goals."

" Okay, come with me," Brie said as she led Jon to her desk.

Jon thought to himself, *if only.*

Jon arrived home a bit after three that afternoon and didn't remember much except that he couldn't stop looking at Brie. He hoped he hadn't made her uncomfortable. Thanks to her help, he had a basic plan for he and Sara, and most of what he envisioned was part of the package. They would see most of Italy south of Rome and spend a lot of time on the Amalfi coast, which was most important to for Selena's ancestors and family.

Next, he would need to see Brie a few more times for the details, and that interested him the most at this moment. He could not recall ever meeting a lady like her in many years and most certainly not a single one.

Perhaps the question was, why single? Maybe she didn't like men, or she had someone in her life, or maybe Jon was just lucky and the timing was right. He was sure he felt a connection when she took his hand in hers to say goodbye. Ho could not help but notice the touch lingered longer than was necessary.

It had been a fantastic day. If Sara were not under the pressure that she was, he would be on the phone to share it all with her.

CHAPTER THIRTEEN

It was early morning, and as usual, Jon was up and having his coffee by 6 a.m. He could see through the window it was beginning to get light. The day so far appeared like it was going to be somewhat cloudy and dreary, which was pretty typical for this time of year. The trees were still bare and the world seemed to be in limbo waiting for spring.

Checking the thermometer, he saw that the temperature was a chilly 44 degrees, also about average for this time of year. It wouldn't be all that long now before he and Sara would be headed off on their adventure. He chatted with Sara last night and as they talked she shared with him that all was well at the office.

She was settling into her new role, and people were finally moving on after the tragedy. She mentioned that she was a bit annoyed that some people's attitudes were so selfish earlier and a few barely recognized the drama, so wrapped up in their own worlds. However, all in all, the firm was going forward as Mr. Evans had wanted.

This morning Jon was looking forward to his next meeting with Brie at the travel agency, and simultaneously not looking forward to another appointment with yet another new doctor. He was not happy having to get comfortable with another doctor, particularly since his last one was a sexy and pretty woman. This was normal with the VA. They moved people around quite a bit; doctors and nurses moved on. He did know in advance that his new doc was a man and hopefully he wouldn't be some young, eager brat just out of medical school. No matter, he supposed. It was time to get the details on his latest battery of tests and find out what his plan needed to be to keep going. He was grateful his first appointment was with Brie. *I would hate to see her after the doc in case I am in a bad mood.*

Jon decided to stop by his favorite Italian bakery and pick up a few croissants with that fantastic and tasty crème filling for all the staff at the travel office. He made a mental note to try one of these in Italy and compare his home version with the real deal.

He noticed Brie, who was chatting with one of the other agents. She spotted him immediately. "Good Morning, Mr. Milo," she said, smiling that beautiful smile.

"Please call me Jon," he said. "After all, I know you well enough to assume it's okay to bring these to everyone." He handed her the bag of goodies.

"So much for my diet," laughed Brie.

Jon quickly and almost regretfully said, "Brie you certainly do not need to diet."

"Why thank you Jon, but a girl has to watch her figure."

That's my job, Jon thought to himself as he noticed how wonderfully tight her dress was. The scoop neckline gave him a magnificent view of her feminine charms. He wondered if she'd dressed this way for their appointment. *Get your mind right old man; she is way out of your league.*

"Jon, I have your final itinerary, along with air, hotel and train paperwork. This trip is going to be a fantastic experience for you both. I suggest you take this all home and go over it and share everything with Sara. If you have any questions, my home telephone and my cell numbers are at the top of the page. Feel free to call me with any changes or issues," Brie offered.

She gave him both her numbers? He wondered if he might read anything into that. Hope soared.

"Thank you so much, Brie. I am sure it's perfect but I will call for sure." Jon promised. Then he went for it. "Perhaps we could have a bite to eat one evening to celebrate this accomplishment?"

Smiling coyly, Brie looked him right in the eye and said, "Yes, Jon that would be lovely. When did you have in mind?"

He was completely taken off guard by this sudden happy turn of events. Nothing like this had ever happened to him and to be honest, he felt a bit tongue-tied.

"Um, how about Saturday evening?" he stammered.

"Fantastic!" Brie said and smiled as she reached out and touched his arm with her hand.

You idiot, you are feeling like a school kid on his first date. Get a grip, he thought. Her hand on his bare arm felt like an electric shock running straight up his sleeve to his brain, giving him a case of the stupids.

"Okay, then about seven would be good?"

"Yes, ideal and here is my address." She handed him a note that she had written in advance of their meeting.

Is it my imagination or was this all planned? Okay, How do I get out of here gracefully? "I look forward to it, and I will see you then. Call me if you change your mind," Jon said, unable to look Brie in those beautiful green eyes.

As Jon left the travel office, he felt like he was walking on air. What the hell just happened? More importantly, how did it happen? Maybe it would be a one-time thing, he thought. After all, she was younger by several years and could likely have any date she wanted. *Okay, Jarhead that is enough negative thinking. Time to gear up and take this challenge head-on. You still have a lot of life to live.*

Jon headed to the VA clinic and arrived realizing he was completely unaware of the trip there. All he could think about was Brie and what Saturday night might bring. The urge to get ahead of himself was hard to resist. It was only a first date, and perhaps all she had in mind was a platonic friendship. Then he remembered her dress. The shortness of it showing off her perfect legs and the scoop neckline intended to share her fantastic cleavage. She certainly had not dressed like that the first three times they had met for trip planning. *Well, Marine, do your best to be a gentleman and remember your manners, the lady has class.* A little soft voice sounded off in his head and he was sure it was Serena. "Okay Jon. What the hell took you so long?" he heard the voice say.

Arriving a few minutes early for his appointment with the new doc, Jon sat waiting with his mind on so many things that had suddenly become part of his life. Sara and their plans, and now there was Brie, and the possibilities that relationship could offer. The largest hurdle to overcome now was his dubious health, which was perhaps the most puzzling and frustrating.

The sudden introduction of Brie into his boring life somehow gave him a burst of courage to face the prognosis of his health and the direction that would take him. *If I don't pay attention to my health I will never have the opportunity for a more meaningful relationship with either of the important women in my life.* No matter the health issues he knew with conviction he would fight to be able to enjoy all the other good in his life as long as possible.

"Sergeant Jon Milo." His name was repeated a second time loudly… "Milo!!!" Brought out of his deep thoughts and into the present, Jon responded with a quick wave and followed the nurse into the examining room where very little was said. She took his vitals and told him the doctor would be in shortly, as if he didn't know the routine by heart.

The door opened and in marched the new guy, a genuine military doctor and quite the opposite of what he expected.

"Good morning Sergeant Milo, I am Dr. Wilson." He smiled broadly with his hand out to welcome Jon to his world. Jon stood and accepted the handshake with a "Good Morning sir." The sir was out of habit; the doc was in uniform and wore the oak leaf insignia for the rank of Commander in the US Navy. Jon was surprised. "Sorry Commander, but this is the first time I have had a military doctor attending me," he said.

"Yes, Sergeant, it is unusual, but I am here as part of the task force assigned to determine the changes necessary to make the VA better for our vets like you. I chose your case because of your history. I do have the results of your tests, and we need to discuss them and a plan for the future."

Jon shifted in his chair, nervous. He finally blurted out, "Okay Commander, what is the diagnosis?"

"Jon…may I call you Jon?" The commander doctor looked at Jon over his glasses for assurance.

"I am honored, sir." Jon responded.

"Jon, I have some good news but also some not so good. Your kidneys are holding steady at stage three, but my biggest concern is your blood pressure. So far it has been somewhat controlled and helped by the medication prescribed, but it also appears you may be developing some areas of blockage. We want to observe you and determine soon if you may need surgery to eliminate any obstructions.

He paged through Jon's chart and continued. "I am also concerned about a shadow that shows in your chest X-ray. It may be nothing but could be something that doesn't belong there. We will do another X-ray in a few weeks, and if there any changes then we will decide the best course of action. I noticed in your file that you quit smoking many years ago. That hasn't changed, has it?" the Doc asked seriously.

"No Doc, it hasn't. I have no interest in smoking and even if I did my daughter would shoot me. Besides, it is so socially unaccecptable now, and well, I may have

a new love interest in my life. Too soon to tell though."
Jon said.

"Well, Sergeant Milo. Just a brief thought, we are
kindred brothers, and although I understand you have
allowed me to be more personal in this relationship,
something we both know to be vital, I will occasionally
slip and refer to you by your rank. Although most people
can't make the distinction, Sergeant is the rank you have
earned for a lifetime, and I will respect that as much as I
respect our growing friendship. Good with you?

"Additionally, I would like you to get a blood pressure monitor for use at home. I will put on in the orders
to the pharmacy will send it to you. I want you to take
your blood pressure each morning when you wake and
each night before you retire. Please make a chart to note
the readings each day. I will want to see that chart when
you return for your tests. If at any time your blood pressure numbers exceed 155 I want you to come to the
emergency room, just to be on the safe side. Is that
clear?" the Commander queried.

"Yes of course, Doc." Jon replied. "Doc, I have a
very personal question to ask you," Jon said, looking
right at the man. "Can I take Viagra safely? I never have
before, but then I may need to know that answer in the
near future."

"Sergeant, I am sure you know how the pill works
and frankly with your blood pressure issues at the

moment I would advise against it. That does not mean never, just not right now."

"Aye-aye Sir," Jon said, grateful for Dr. Wilson's candor and attitude. His behavior seemed more like that of a warrior, a tested military man and a protagonist against disease and injury.

"Let's get together again in four weeks and get a couple of tests done and see where that takes us. Okay by you?" the doc asked.

"Yes sir, that works for me." Jon replied. He rose to leave. Extending their hands again, the men said their goodbyes. Sergeant Milo knew he had a friend defending him in their dual foxhole.

"He's got my back," Jon said out loud as he walked to his car. While it seemed his body might be falling apart he knew he'd just have to take it one day at a time. Meanwhile, he had a date with a goddess to look forward to on Saturday night. *You lucky asshole*, he laughed to himself.

CHAPTER FOURTEEN

The phones were ringing on almost every line in every office, and Congressman Platt was trying very hard to concentrate on a speech he was planning to give at his nest committee meeting. "Leslie," he called to his executive assistant. "What the hell is going on in here? Why are the phones going crazy?" the Congressman asked, irritated by the distraction.

Leslie came in the door, obviously flustered. "Congressman, you called?" she asked.

"Yes, I did. What is happening? These phones are out of control."

Closing the door, Leslie tried to explain. "Most of the calls are the media trying to get answers and a chance to talk to you. Some are also constituents that want the same thing." Leslie explained in detail.

"Okay, but what do they want to talk to me about?" he asked.

"Well apparently there is a new scandal or rumor of a scandal being leaked, and it concerns one of your friends." Leslie explained.

"Okay and just who would that be?" the Congressman asked, still confused.

Leslie hesitated at being the bearer of bad news. She did not want to be the messenger that got shot. "Jeremiah Evans is who, Congressman."

"Jeremiah, really? What on earth could the rumors be about?" he asked with some irritation.

"Apparently some sources say Mr. Evans was involved with some bad people and his accident was not an accident. That is all I know at the moment. It's all still very sketchy, and the media is like a wild pack of wolves on a blood trail. They are looking for any bit of information they can find, even if it is just rumor."

"This has to be bullshit. Get the Police Commissioner on the phone and/or the Mayor, whoever is first available, now, please. I want some answers. Jeremiah was a close friend, and I need to know if his death was not an accident."

Congressman Platt came up the hard way. He went to public schools and paid his way through a small college in the Northeast. His family was a blue-collar, working-class family. His intelligence and hard work ethic had served him well in his career, which was never intended to be politics. He went to school as a business major with intentions of working at the highest levels in corporate America. Shortly after his career began, he was involved in a heavily contested property takeover, and his beliefs forced him to break off from his employer and campaign on behalf of the people who the acquisition would harm.

As his popularity rose in the media with his successful blocking of the issues, the state political party people came to him and asked him to seek election to Congress. They were correct that his charming good looks and his grounded ideals would make him a strong candidate. The vote was a landslide in his favor, and he began his political career twelve years ago. His popularity continued to grow, and his hard work on behalf of the people of New York made him virtually unbeatable by any other candidate. He was plain speaking and yet very polished in all circles of society. He had the talent to speak with a longshoreman on his level or a society debutante. Everyone wanted to be acquainted with the Congressman. His best-kept secret wasn't scandalous; he loved to ride his Harley on weekends when he wasn't in Washington.

Leslie opened the door part way to tell the Congressman she had the commissioner on the line.

"Mr. Commissioner, please tell me what the hell is happening. Is there a substantial reason to believe that Jeremiah Evans accident was not an accident?" the Congressman demanded.

"Congressman, you know I can't share details. However, I can tell you the accident is under investigation. When we have concluded the process, I will read you in. I wish I could tell you more, but we are really trying to keep a tight lid on this from the media. Rumors could hurt the investigation. I'm not sure how the media frenzy got started to begin with, but for now, please tell any media who contact you that all you know is that the accident of your friend is under investigation. If you would refer all questions to our public affairs office that would be helpful," the Commissioner explained.

"Of course Commissioner, but what do I tell his associates and family? Are you looking into his law firm as well?" Platt asked.

"Again, Congressman, there is little I can tell you except that all avenues are open to us right now. We will not let this take any longer than necessary," the commissioner assured him.

"All right. Thank you for telling me what you can. Please keep me in the loop and call me anytime day or night if more developments happen."

Congressman Platt hung up and called out to his assistant. "Leslie, get Sara Milo on the line for me, please."

The Congressman quickly saw the light blinking and grabbed the receiver. "Good Morning, Sara, how are you?" he asked.

"Good Morning Devon," Sara responded. "What can I do for you?"

"Sara, it appears that rumors are floating around about Jeremiah and his accident. Have you been contacted by anyone regarding this?" Devon asked.

"Yes, we have," Sara said. "The media is trying desperately to get some responses from any of the staff here. I have put out a directive that no one is to talk to any media about anything. We will maintain a position of ignorance until otherwise notified by the authorities."

"Wise move," the Congressman responded. "I wish I knew more myself, but I don't. I am quite confident all will work out. Jeremiah was a good man. I can't picture him being involved in anything improper."

"Neither can we," Sara agreed. "But as a lawyer, I also know often facts are open to interpretation, and that's what worries me. I need to find out what legal team is on this case then maybe I'll have a higher level of comfort."

Devon Platt paused, then blurted, "Sara, not that this is the best time, but it is something I have been wanting to do since the Christmas party. Would you care to have dinner with me one night this week while I am in town, before I head back to DC?"

Sara thought, *okay there it is finally. This hunk of a guy not only in looks but also in intellect is interested. What is his agenda? Why me, I am certainly not a power broker that a politician would be interested in.* Suddenly her mouth went dry, and her ability to speak was leaving on a jet plane. Why on earth would that thought from a song come into her mind?

Gathering herself, she responded. "That would be lovely. Where and what time?"

"I'm not sure about your dining preferences, but I can recommend a very relaxing place with fantastic food, unpretentious. How about the Gotham Bar and Grill at Union Square at 8 pm Friday night? The dress is somewhat casual, so be comfortable," he offered.

"That sounds wonderful Devon. I will see you there. Thank you," Sara said.

"Perhaps I'll have a bit more information by then but until then stay strong and support your people," advised the Congressman.

"I will and thank you for your concerns," Sara said, disconnecting the call.

Sara thought casual and comfortable would be perfect. He was entirely down to earth for someone so powerful. She smiled. Could he be the real deal? She had just two days to wait to learn more. For now, damage control in the firm was the task at hand. She needed to call a meeting of the partners to discuss how the firm should handle this situation. More importantly, they needed to look internally to see if there was anything that would expose the firm to vulnerability.

CHAPTER FIFTEEN

It seemed to Jon that time had been moving in slow motion while he waited for Saturday night to arrive. Now that it was here, a mild state of panic had set in. An evening with a lovely lady that came into his life from seemingly out of nowhere was certainly a reason to be more than a bit nervous. He needed a plan for what to wear and more importantly where to take the lovely lady on their date.

No doubt part of the panic was the realization he would need to have a conversation as well. He had two levels of concern. First, it had been many years since he had the need to have a meaningful conversation with anyone except Sara. Second, Jon was worried she might ask too many questions that he was not ready to answer yet, if ever. Maybe he could focus on asking her questions and listen to the answers and keep the attention on her and off himself. *That way I can't put my foot in my mouth too badly and ruin this before it even starts.*

As far as what to wear, apparently she liked what she saw both times they met so maybe it was not as important. If his old junk of a truck didn't scare Brie away, then he figured the clothes wouldn't matter much. He reminded himself to polish his shoes and put some creases in his pants.

As he drove to Brie's home, he wondered what she was like outside the office. Where was she from initially, was she married before? Did she have any children, or family nearby? What kind of music did she like? How did she feel about military men, and perhaps most importantly what was her religious affiliation, if any? Suddenly Jon realized he had a lot to talk about and slowly he began to feel comfortable and confident that he could make it through the evening. He knew he would have to guard against sounding like he was interrogating Brie and remember to listen to her answers with real interest. He was sure he'd commit the interesting details to memory.

At the last moment before he turned the corner to her street he thought for a moment about Serena and how would she feel about this. Probably her only comment would be, *it's about time.* As he got closer to the address, he began to notice the neighborhood was a step up from his. The houses were bigger with large yards and very upscale cars in the driveways. Christmas decorations still lit up the street.

Apparently, these people subscribed to Selena's view on decorations, but it was past New Years, so maybe they had been too busy to take them them all down yet. He couldn't help but notice that most of the decorations were put up by pros. The lighting on the two-story houses went to the roof peaks. Even he wouldn't climb a ladder that damn high so they must have used lifts.

Looking for the house numbers, he eventually found Brie's home. It was a two-story garrison, well appointed, and like all the others around her, still decorated. The driveway was freshly refinished, and the house appeared to be well maintained. By the looks of the front door, which was solid wood with cut glass in the center, as well as beautiful glass sidelights, no question this house was expensive and well constructed. Just then another question popped into his mind for later.

He shut off his old truck and the engine shuddered and finally stopped running, but during the process, it was pretty noisy. He hoped Brie didn't hear that noise. Maybe it was time to get some new wheels. The old beater owed him nothing, according to Sara anyway.

Before he even reached the door, Brie had it opened and was smiling a huge smile that completely disarmed Jon. Her dress was incredible. Short to be sure, which was ideal because her legs were perfect, and tight fitting as her weight was apparently suitable for her height. Her hair was in a casual ponytail that made her look even younger. She wore a very delicate but obviously expensive necklace that seemed to point the way to the fertile valley of cleavage her dress revealed. Last but not least were her shoes. This lady had excellent taste from top to bottom. *What the hell does she want with me?*

"Good evening Brie," Jon stammered, a bit self-conscious.

Getting closer Brie came to him and planted a delicate kiss on his cheek. "Welcome and good evening to you. Please, come in," Brie invited.

Jon stepped into the tastefully decorated home and could not help notice how warm and comfortable everything was. He immediately felt at ease.

Brie suggested that before they left perhaps a cocktail to begin the evening. "That would be wonderful," he responded, grateful she had taken the lead.

Brie offered, "Please get comfortable, and I will be right back."

Jon removed his coat and began to look around. He saw some photographs of what could be a daughter and husband and grandchildren but no pictures of any men her age. As Jon walked by the bookcase, he came upon a framed document hanging on the wall. The contents held what appeared to be a commendation with Brie's name on it, with a Marine Corps logo in the center of the heading. Not having his glasses handy he couldn't really tell what it was about. *My God*, he thought, *is she a Marine? Is this really possible?* He admonished himself to wait and let her volunteer the information in the conversation if she chose to. This was not a subject for him to delve into yet anyway.

Moving across the room, he stood by the picture window. He looked out and wondered what this night would be like just as Brie came back into the room with a beer for him and a glass of wine for herself. *This lady can read minds. Damn, I need to be careful.*

"How did you know I prefer a good beer over wine? " he asked as he accepted the glass.

"Honestly I took a wild guess and made an assumption. Was I correct?" she asked with a smile.

"Yes you were, and I find that so thoughtful that you would take the time to even think about that. Truthfully no matter what you brought back I would have been fine with your choice."

Brie gestured to the sofa in the living room and offered Jon a seat. As they sat, Jon could not help but notice that there was very little space between them and he could even feel the heat from her thigh pressed against his. The thoughts that raced through his mind made him feel like he was back in high school on a first date. *Hey, knucklehead, cool your jets. This lady is a lady.*

After the first beer, another was suddenly in his hand, and the clock was moving faster than he could imagine. They had been chatting for close to two hours and no mention of dinner. "Brie excuse me for bringing this up but shouldn't we leave for the restaurant and have dinner?"

Brie responded, "You're right we probably should but, I have an idea. What would you think about staying here for dinner? I wouldn't even mind if we ordered a pizza. I really like chatting with you without other people around. Would that be okay?" she asked flirtatiously

"Yes of course whatever you want is fine with me," he told Brie. He thought this would be more than fine, and after all, he wouldn't have to apologize for his truck.

"Wonderful," she said, heading to get her phone. "What do you like on it?"

"I'm good with anything as long as no onions," Jon said.

"No onions is a good idea for a first date," she said, barely loud enough for him to hear. "Ok, I'll order it now. Should take about forty-five minutes."

After the pizza arrived, the discussions about their lives and past continued. Jon shared that he was a Viet Nam vet and had some health issues connected but no details and Brie shared that she had been married but was divorced many years ago from a man who turned out to be an abysmal choice. The only good thing that came from her marriage was her daughter Brianna and now her amazing grandchildren, a boy named Dale and a little girl Sophia; they lived in Florida.

The conversations continued about music, politics and even religion. Jon was amazed at how much they had in common on these subjects. He found himself daydreaming a bit about what their second date could be like if in fact she wanted a second one.

Jon looked at his watch and midnight was approaching. It was definitely the latest he had been awake in several years. Jon made the decision to gracefully broach the subject of leaving and began thanking Brie for a beautiful evening.

As Jon reached for his coat and headed for the door, he turned and asked Brie, "Could we do this again, soon perhaps?"

Instead of speaking, Brie moved close to Jon and leaned in and touched her full lips to his and began a passionate kiss which seemed to last forever. His mind whirled in emotions, and he let his arms encircle her tiny waist. Brie was on her tiptoes as she had taken off her high heels long ago. Now their bodies melted together and the message was clear. This was just the beginning.

As Jon stumbled down the steps from the emotions of the moment, towards his truck, he looked back over his shoulder at the lovely vision named Brie. She smiled and said goodbye in two words. "Call me."

The ride home was a blur with all that was going on in his head. One thing for sure, he wanted more, much more. He really had wanted to say Semper Fi to her, but that would wait for another time of her choosing.

CHAPTER SIXTEEN

Friday morning Sara stood frozen in her closet, trying to decide what on earth to wear to the office that would also be appropriate for her date this evening with the Congressman. She decided that layering would solve the issue. A pantsuit and heels along with a white blouse that could later be a bit unbuttoned for a more casual look and she would take along a sweater in case a chill was in the air.

The morning air was quite brisk, and the unexpected sunshine made the option of walking part way to the office inviting. However, checking her watch, she hailed a taxi instead. This morning was going to be most likely tricky with the happenings and investigation of the death of Mr. Evans. She also needed to find out if Mrs. Evans was able to have visitors yet.

The cab driver had a radio tuned to some sports show. The topic was a very loud and at-odds discussion about the upcoming Super Bowl. Sara wished all she had to worry about was a football game. What was it about a game where men try to do their best to knock each other senseless? It had been part of society going back to the Romans with the gladiators. Why were humans so bloodthirsty?

Enough of the little thoughts, she admonished herself. There was much to do at the office this morning. Was it really possible that Mr. Evans was involved in something that could have gotten him killed? That just didn't seem likely but then Sara knew from being an attorney that it was hard to really know anyone and what they could be capable of. Again the Congressman came to mind.

Sara arrived a bit early to the office as planned and just like always, Victoria had come to work even earlier to prepare for the partners meeting that would happen first thing. "Good morning Victoria, you are in early."

"Yes, I am but sure not far in front of you. Are you ready for the meeting?"

"I sure hope I am. Do you have the documents I requested?" Sara asked.

"Yes, they are on your desk and here is your coffee," said Victoria with a smile.

Taking a sip of coffee Sara opened the file Victoria had put together. It contained a list of clients and litigations Mr. Evans had recently been involved with as well as older clients going back five years. The file also included email records for the past twelve months, which had to be handled carefully because of the attorney-client privilege issue. Sara was quite confident that nothing would be discovered that was inappropriate or illegal in any way. Mr. Evans had been an attorney for many years with an unblemished record in all areas as far as she was aware.

She spent the next hour and a half going through the in-depth file prepared by Victoria and could find nothing suspicious. Closing the file, Sara breathed a sigh of relief. If something was wrong she was not the one to discover it and would have nothing uncomfortable to report to the other partners. As best she could tell they would have to wait for the police to complete their investigation and deal with whatever might come from that.

When Sara entered the conference room, she could sense the mood was one of paranoia and uncertainty. Sara took her seat at the table for the first time and could not help feel the eyes that followed her every move. Sara knew she had no reason to feel anything but secure and confident.

She had always worked hard, minded her own business and avoided making many enemies and most importantly, always made sure all professional relationships were just that, professional.

Mr. Mason called the meeting to order for all five partners, three of which were named partners. Named partners were the lawyers in the firm who had their names on the door. Sara was the newest, so now the firm name was Mason, Davis, and Milo. It had a beautiful ring to it but sadly some of the people answering the phone still said Evans, Mason and Davis, Attorneys at Law. It would take time for the change to be natural. Sara had been expecting some backlash from the other partners that might have been expecting to have their name on the door but so far none had materialized. That really surprised her with human nature being what it was. Maybe time would reveal those feelings at some point and most likely it was way in the background, considering the tragedy and circumstances. She reminded herself to be careful and observant in the near future.

The agenda was a simple one-item agenda: to determine the vulnerability of the firm with regards to any suspicions by the police and perhaps the media once the story breaks.

Mr. Mason began. "Does anyone have any information that is pertinent to the situation this firm is in at this time?"

No one spoke up for a few minutes, and then Sara offered to share what she had learned by examining the files that were currently being handled by Mr. Evans. "Gentlemen, I have personally been through all of the client lists and current litigations that Mr. Evans was working on, and at this moment I am not able to find anything that would lead to any suspicious activities of any kind.

"We don't have a lot of information at this point from the police so I suggest that until we have more to work with we should operate in a business as usual posture. We should let all of the staff know that if anyone approaches them for information, they should report it immediately to me. I am willing to be the point of contact for the police and the media. Of course, I will keep you all up to date on any developments. I will also try to speak with Mrs. Evans when she is well enough for a visitor, but I would doubt she would have any knowledge that we do not."

"I think that is an excellent approach for the time being Sara, Thank you for your diligence on this sensitive matter," said Mr. Mason. "With that being said are we all in agreement with this plan?" Mr. Mason asked.

The partners all voted aye and the meeting was adjourned.

Sara went immediately back to her office to deal with the usual issues that were starting to pile up on her desk. A knock on her office door brought Sara back to the present as she was thinking about her Dad once again. Victoria came bounding in with a cheerful attitude that often Sara found annoying, but that was not Vic's fault.

"Hey, boss. Don't you have a date tonight?"

Without looking up, Sara answered, "I have a dinner meeting that's what I have, so don't make assumptions that are not real."

"Okay, if you say, so," Victoria said, smirking as she backed out of the office and closed the door.

Sara chuckled when she saw Vic exit. *Poor girl, she so wants me to get a man. Well, just maybe I will,* she thought, banging her fist on the desk. *I still need to know his secret. I am very sure he has one or more.*

It was about 7:30 and Sara was in her taxi on her way to the restaurant. The realization that she was having dinner with the Congressman suddenly brought on a "hot flash" that she was not used to. She wanted to get information about her dad, but she also didn't want him thinking that was the only reason she was having dinner with him. She'd have to try to let him take the lead. That should not be a problem, as he owned a strong personality. She suspected he was very accustomed to having people pay attention when he spoke. Most likely he was used to leading the conversation.

Just before the taxi arrived, Sara remembered she needed to make herself appear more casual. She immediately removed the scarf she had worn with her pantsuit and blouse and stuffed it into her rather large Coach bag, a gift to herself when she was appointed name partner. She carefully unbuttoned her blouse just enough to look casual but not trashy.

Maybe trashy would come later, she giggled to herself. She looked down at her chest and saw that she had just the right amount of reveal but at that moment realized that she was pale white and she really needed to take a vacation to the islands and get herself tanned up. She did not like the electric beaches in the city and had stopped going to them quite some time ago.

The taxi came to a sudden halt like they always did in the city and the cabbie said, "Here we are Miss. That will be $8.75."

Sara handed the driver a twenty and at first started to wait for change but changed her mind and got out of the cab and headed to the restaurant door.

Entering any restaurant in New York one could expect a cacophony of sounds. Dishes clattering, loud conversations, the shaker and blenders by the bartender making the perfect cocktail; all familiar sounds that told Sara this was a busy and well-liked place. The variety of conversations with a wide array of accents and languages let the newcomer know that this was a familiar hangout; they were comfortable so she should be, too.

The decor was a bit surprising to Sara. Not that she didn't like it, but that this was the choice of the

Congressman. The dark wood bar back, the bright lights along with the televisions over the bar showing various sports in progress just didn't strike her as a place a Congressman would prefer. She did like the high ceilings and the chandeliers in the main dining room. Perhaps he was more man than a legend in his own mind, unlike most politicians. That would be refreshing.

Sara looked around the dining area and saw the Devon standing and waving her towards him. She noticed that he was wearing a casual sports coat with an open collar white shirt, so in fact all he had done after his workday was to remove his tie. Edging her way towards him, she noticed she caught several glances from men and even some women as she made her way to her man of the hour. When she got to the table, the Congressman extended his hand for a handshake and pulled her chair out for her to be seated. The table was quite small, but in New York, that was common, to seat as many people as possible.

"Good evening, Sara, you look terrific," the Congressman said with a bit of a leer.

"Why thank you, Congressman, you are not so bad either." Sara thought quickly, *is that the best you got? Good grief!*

"Okay, let's get something settled if it's okay with you. Please call me Devon and not Congressman. Deal?"

"That's a deal but only when we are not in a group of others," Sara suggested.

"That's fine with me, for now. I do understand your concern." Devon replied. "However tonight I would like to get to know you better and leave shop talk out of the evening."

"That sounds perfect," Sara said, with a broad smile meant to interest the Congressman.

The conversations began lightly enough about schools they had attended, parents, upbringing and all the other get-to-know-you topics. During the early chatter, Sara couldn't help notice that occasionally Devon's eyes were looking well below hers and for some reason that was just fine. She felt gratified that he was looking at her like a woman and not a colleague.

Sara resisted the temptation to say, "Okay Devon, my eyes are up here," but that would be mean and not necessary as the number of buttons she undid were serving the purposed intended. She could not stop looking into his eyes, when they didn't stray. Even his voice Sara found mesmerizing. *Oh, dear girl, you are headed for some trouble*, she admonished herself. *Maybe it's about time.*

Sara did want to get to her fathers' issue at some point, so she deduced now would be better than later. "Devon, Can I ask if any progress has been made for my father to receive the recognition he deserves?" she asked quietly.

"Sara, I can only tell you that at this point your request is on the list for the top brass in the Marine Corps Awards Department. When will it be finalized or decided, I don't know at this time; I doubt that anyone does. Those old wheels turn rather slowly, I'm sorry to say. I will, however, make an inquiry that just might give them a sense of urgency," Devon offered. "Please keep in mind that the Marine Corps in particular is very picky when it comes to awarding high level medals to anyone."

"I would hope they are," Sara offered. "I know I may have a problem getting Dad to agree to accept any recognition. He simply does not think go himself a hero." Sara shared.

"Sara, may I ask you a question about your dad?" Devon said with a serious tone.

"Yes, of course," she said.

"Do you know if he *wants* to be reminded about that time in his life? The reason I ask is, a while back there was similar case, and that soldier would not accept any sort of honor. For some, it just is too painful, I guess."

"Devon, you could be right. Dad doesn't know I'm trying to do this for him and I'm sure he doesn't know his men reached out to me. I just haven't decided to tell him yet, because if it doesn't come through I may never tell him."

Looking around Sara noticed that most of the customers were gone. She thought she did not want this evening to end but considering Devon's political position that he should be a man of caution. Her expectations would be that if a relationship was on the horizon, it was likely that the progression will be slow, which also met her needs for the time being. Her focus for the near future had to be her new position at the firm and her father.

"Devon, I'm a believer that everyone has some secret that they do not typically share with everyone and I am quite sure you are no different. So if I ask you what your best kept secret is, would you share it with me?"

To say Devon was shocked would be an understatement. "Sara, my personal life and my professional life are always open to scrutiny by everyone. That's most often by the press but also by political opponents. However, there is one thing I have managed to keep private and I trust you will keep my confidence," he said seriously.

Sara looked at him with concern and strong curiosity. "Yes of course, Devon as long as it's not illegal," she offered.

Devon laughed loudly. "I assure you it's not illegal but could be considered way out of character for a US Congressman. Whenever I can, usually once in a while on weekends I like to hit the road on my Harley with other friends who are also on the QT. I guess you could say I am a closet biker," he admitted.

Sara was certainly taken by surprise. That was not even on her radar in a guy who presented himself as straight-laced, well dressed and so professional. He had to be joking. "You are kidding me, right?" Sara asked hopefully.

"Not at all. I bought the bike just before I ran for office and then once I was elected I decided, why shouldn't do what I enjoy? I love the open road. I like the relationships I have developed with other riders and they for the most part also have everyday lives that don't fit the fantasy. We don't do drugs or anything. We just love the feeling of freedom that comes from heading down new roads without worrying about appearances and judgments. You should try it sometime, you might be surprised," Devon suggested.

Sara was immediately envisioning herself on the back of his motorcycle, holding on to him tightly with the wind in her hair and the feeling of the motor and the road in her thighs.

"Okay, when?" Sara blurted out, surprising herself and Devon.

"How about tomorrow? I'll pick you up in the morning and we'll cruise the New Jersey countryside down towards the shore. It will be a bit chilly so dress warm but it will also be exhilarating. I have a second helmet that should fit you just fine," he assured her.

Sara thought for a moment and could see no way out of this, nor did she really want one. She did wonder why he had a second helmet so handy. Who was the last one to wear it? "What does one wear for a motorcycle ride this time of year? Long underwear?" she asked with a giggle.

"That's a good start." Devon said. "You will also need a scarf and warm gloves. Boots and heavy socks are a big help too."

"Ok I think I have all that but I can't imagine it being very fashionable," Sara laughed.

"Fashionable is not the goal, you can save that for spring and summer. Tomorrow is about staying warm," Devon reminded her.

Now they were the only two left in the place and it was time to go. The waiters were beginning to hover to send them the message that it was time to leave. Waiters in New York City were not exactly subtle when it was time to close.

"Sara, I have enjoyed this evening so much, and I am looking forward to tomorrow," he said, touching her hand ever so gently while looking into her eyes.

Sara returned the gaze and said, "I am as well. It is certainly a bit of a surprise but I know you understand my priorities for the immediate future. I want to thank you for sharing your secret life with me. I value openness and honesty above most everything else.

"I am also looking forward to our adventure but please be patient with me. I have never been on a motorcycle before. You do obey speed limits. Right?" Sara asked.

Walking out of the restaurant Devon hailed a cab and they both climbed in and headed for Sara's brownstone. The ride was quiet as Sara examined her feelings. She assumed Devon was doing the same. After a short moment Devon took her hand in his, and with the help of the streetlights, Sara could see a smile on his face and a heartfelt look of admiration, which surprised her for sure. No need to enter into small talk at this moment. The mutual touch was saying all that needed to be said.

The cab pulled up to Sara's place, and Devon got out and asked the cabbie to wait. Like the gentleman she expected him to be, he took her arm and walked her up the stairs to the big front door of the building.

Sara used her key to open the outer door and without a word turned and gently kissed Devon while putting her arms around his neck. He responded, and although there was just the right amount of passion, there was also a very real holding back as there should have been considering their positions and professional relationship.

Breaking the almost chaste kiss Sara smiled and said, "Thank you for a beautiful evening Devon, and I will see you in the morning." Turning for the door, she looked over her shoulder as Devon got into the cab and with a quick wave was down the street.

Sara began her nightly ritual of getting ready for bed, distracted by the events of the evening. *This man is real* she thought to herself. *He is self-made and not a member of the lucky sperm club. He is honest, intelligent for sure, self-confident and most certainly very attractive.* As she climbed into bed, she imagined that tomorrow would be an adventure unlike any she had ever had. Her last thought before falling fast asleep was that she'd need to find her long johns in the morning.

CHAPTER
SEVENTEEN

The late October night was about as dark as could be. The rainy season was torturing everyone on duty and off and with this weather. No moon, just the miserable pissing rain that never really seemed to come down yet soaked everyone and everything. Cpl. Milo thought to himself, *this weather is Charlie's kind of night. The rain doesn't bother them at all, and it seems to me the bastards love it. Charlie can crawl for hours if necessary through the wet and the mud and the thick jungle and not let the bugs or anything bother them. This enemy is about as formidable as an enemy could be, and many of these young Marines just don't get it yet.*

As a squad leader responsible for twelve men or more the only job in his mind was to make sure they all got home safe. On a night like this, they needed to be ready for anything. Jon had had the men put out additional tripwires in front of the positions. Some of the trip wires were for grenades and others were for flares that would launch into the sky and illuminate everything and everyone including themselves. Stringing C-Ration cans with pebbles in them also provided additional warnings if moved by man or animal. Fortunately, their area wasn't rife with the damn rock apes of other parts of Viet Nam. Through their curiosity, the plentiful creatures managed to set off trip wires most every night on the Marines defensive perimeters in the hills and mountains where they lived, or so Jon had heard from other outfits.

He looked at his watch, 2:15 am. It was time to get out to the positions and make sure all the holes are on alert especially more alert on a night like this. Jon's spot was in a hole about 40 yards behind the line where he could be in touch with the company commander by field telephone. To reach each man, he would have to slowly make his way to each position and check on the men.

The crazy part of this for Jon was that even as a youngster he was afraid of the dark and now as a man here in Viet Nam he was not only in a dark place, but deadly as well. It required all the courage he could muster to make his way in the darkness to the positions he had put his men. The password for the night was turkey, responded to by stuffing as Thanksgiving was a few weeks away and both were easy for the men to remember. He would need to remind each man that if a flare went off to close their targeting eye quickly and not look at the flash. Closing the one eye retained the night vision for that eye; once the flare went out they wouldn't be completely blinded.

He knew he had a good squad and that each man would look after the other, but the reality was they had not been tested yet. But then neither had he. His biggest fear was that he might let his men down.

After he made the rounds, he was satisfied that all was ready and whatever happened their chances were good. He needed to catch some sleep himself, so it was time to wake up Roselli and let him take over the field phone. Rest never came easy these nights, but it was necessary.

"Roselli, it is your turn to man the field phone. Wake up, Marine." Milo said, as he shook the young boot. Roselli had only been "in country" for a few weeks but had quickly fit in with the squad, even with his bullshit stories of all his women. After all, the kid was only 19, so how much love life experience could he have? Most of the men knew he was full of it, but no one minded; he was a great storyteller.

"Ok, Corporal, I'm awake. Got you covered. I need to slide out of this hole for a piss. I'll be quiet, unless you want me to do it in here?"

"Hurry and be damn quiet. This is Charlie's kind of night," Milo reminded the young Marine.

When Roselli crawled back into their hole, Cpl. Milo reminded him, with a soft whisper, that if the shit did hit the fan, he was to take the extra ammo cans to positions three and seven for the machine guns. "I will be calling in artillery fire orders based on the tracer activity. Do your job, and you'll be fine. Wake me in two hours."

Jon's last thoughts before drifting off to sleep were about going home. *Damn, I miss so many things.*

Jon had barely dropped off to sleep with his poncho pulled over his head when he heard the pop of a flare not far from his position. Jumping up to a kneeling position he could see the jungle in front of the perimeter and there was indeed enemy movement in the tall grass. Just then the perimeter positions began firing heavily but disciplined, a good start, he thought. Reaching for the field phone, he called the company commander and reported they had enemy activity in front of the line and were taking fire. He also asked that artillery fire begin immediately on the pre-designated positions left and center of their location.

Once he received confirmation that his alert was received, Jon headed towards his squads' positions taking the fire. Running full speed, he saw Roselli grab the ammo cans and work his way to his assigned area. Good boy, he thought, pretty cool under fire. No panic in him so far.

Jon went from position to position, shouting out to each man. "Shoot when you have a target. Conserve ammo as much as possible." Jon then launched a parachute flare to let everyone see what was happening in front of them and there about 75 yards in front of them were dozen of black pajama-wearing assholes, most of them armed with AK-47's and RPG's.

Jon went to the automatic weapons positions and directed their fire towards the groups that had the RPG's. As he was continuing to direct fire, he realized that his position number two was not firing at all and he sensed they were in trouble. Rushing to the spot, he saw one of his Marines was wounded, and the other man assigned to the post was shooting with one hand and holding a field dressing on the neck of his partner.

"Need some help here?" he yelled at the young Marine.

"Fucking right I do, Jerry here is bleeding like shit, and I only have one hand."

"Okay, Marine, you keep him from bleeding out, I'll keep the gooks off your back," Milo yelled over the noise of the firefight.

Charlie must have thought they would have better luck on the right side of the line, Jon could see the attack in front had ceased, but now the right side of the line was opening up with auto and rifle fire as the point of attack shifted.

Jon thought to himself, *I need to get my ass over there.* He took off at a run while trying to stay low. On the way, Jon took one man from each of the positions to support the right side of the line. Charlie would be in for a surprise. Each man jumped into a foxhole and started firing at the oncoming targets.

Jon wondered why they didn't have any mortars coming at them. Perhaps this was just a test of the perimeter. Maybe the real attack would happen somewhere else, or else tonight they were only local Cong and didn't yet have the big stuff.

All of a sudden everything went quiet. The night became silent, no flares going off, no shooting, nothing. It was like a bad dream. Jon said to no one in particular, "Well, Charlie certainly knows where we are now. I need to get everyone to other positions and find out if we lost anyone or how many wounded we have."

It would be daylight soon, so most likely Charlie was back in their village and already changed out of their black pajamas. Probably getting ready for work tomorrow. *There's no fucking way we can win this war on their turf. Damn idiot politicians.*

As the relief platoon arrived for the day perimeter assignment, Jon gathered his men. They had been lucky. Only one wounded and no dead. He was proud of his men. They had handled themselves very well. The aftermath of the battle would be hitting Jon and his men quickly. The adrenaline would dissipate and the realization of what they just went through for the first time would become a reality.

Jon felt like it was a time to mourn more than anything. A time to mourn the loss of his innocence, the loss of his humanity that would change him forever and the loss of his youth. Today, he became in many ways an old man, a man who no longer believed in the basics of humans being kind to each other. Of the human race being intolerant of differences. And perhaps the saddest thing of all to a man who was raised as he was, the loss of faith in his government. He knew down deep that at the other end of his rifle were men who had the same hopes of returning to their families and surviving. He couldn't help thinking that if he were defending his home; he would also fight as they do. Again he asked himself, *what the fuck are we doing here?*

The question became overwhelming to Jon. But he also knew that no matter the reasons his only focus was to survive and to do his best to see that his men survived as well. The rest of the whys would have to wait until much later. If he thought about all of that he could lose focus on his only real mission.

Because he was a good Marine and a good citizen he would do his duty, but he was committed to his primary focus on survival. He owed that to his men and his family. He determined at that moment in time to do his best not to let the politicians kill him or his men.

For some, the night would have a profound effect. For others, particularly those who tended to put on a big macho act when faced with adversity, they would bury this trauma deep inside and not admit the permanent effect on their lives. Jon's moment of stark terror came once he completed a head count and knew where each of his men was. He was also in no small degree proud of the fact that he was able to keep his head and get his men in the right place to defend their positions and keep casualties to a bare minimum. He also knew down deep that tonight something changed in him and his men. None of them would ever be the same again.

As he was picking up his gear the Platoon Leader Lt. Murray signaled him over. "Corporal Milo, I need you to take over as platoon Sergeant. Staff Sergeant Plonski was hit pretty bad and most likely will be heading stateside. You will need to name a replacement for yourself as the squad leader. Let me know who you choose, and I will make sure the stripes go with the choice. By the way, you are now Sergeant Milo. Get your new chevrons from the company office. The paperwork will be out shortly."

Jon thought to himself, *Jesus Christ like I don't have enough to worry about already. Now I have a whole damn platoon, that's not good.*

Jon's regular alarm rang and brought him out of the dream of the past. HE felt the cold sheets soaked with sweat on his back and his heart was pounding. The dreams had been haunting him for many years and try as he might he could not predict when he would dream or what would trigger them. Jon knew this one was the most benign one that kept coming back. The dream that he feared the most had no ending or explanation to it in his mind. That made it the worst of all.

Stripping the sweat-soaked sheets off his bed to put into the washing machine he thought, *why couldn't I dream about Brie? That would be a whole lot more fun.*

Getting going in the morning after one of these recurring dreams was always a bit of a chore. It used to be a lot easier when he had work on his mind or decisions to make to care for his family. Now that he was retired with more time to think about the past it became tougher each time. It was just him, and the reminders of the past were ever present.

Filling up the washing machine with his bedding brought an act of cleansing. *If only I could wash away the past and the memories of a time best forgotten this easily.* It wasn't that he didn't want to hold onto the memory of the men he served with, but the reality was that he had significant difficulty remembering them without remembering the bad shit that happened.

In fact, there were very few names he could recall at all and that brought him additional guilt he carried all these years. How could he not know every name from that time? The times were wrong, but the guys were great and deserved better from their leader. For some reason, he remembered Roselli very well and his radio man Nathan…but not his last name. Jon knew he should have answered his letters and phone calls. Maybe soon. He understood when he first came home that he should expect some survivor's guilt and he accepted that. The questions he wanted answers to were what happened to him. How was he injured? Did he not take care of his men? Did he let them down? Tough questions, he thought. He wasn't sure he ever wanted the answers, but didn't understand how it was possible that no one could tell him so long ago.

Jon made his cup of strong coffee and walked out the front door to find his paper. His pain in the ass newspaper kid always did his best to throw it anyplace other than somewhere near the door. *I guess I should be grateful that I still have home delivery.* It probably wouldn't last much longer; he kept getting requests from the local paper to subscribe online. *Hell no, I like the newspaper in my hands, the smell, the touch of the newsprint all part of an era almost gone. A bit sad, but I will continue as long as it is possible.*

Jon finally found his paper in the bush beside the front porch. He walked back into the house and headed to his favorite chair. Putting his coffee cup on the small table beside his chair and kicking off his shoes he put his feet up on the ottoman. Unfolding the paper to the front page nothing at first glance grabbed his attention, as usual.

Glancing out the window, he saw neighbors driving by on their way to work, and his thoughts turned to his daughter Sara. She now had new responsibilities and increased status in her firm, and he wondered how she was doing. No doubt she could handle anything that came her way, she always had been able to. This thought process took him to thoughts about their upcoming trip in the spring to Italy and what was he going to say to her about the past and those issues that she was curious about, and in particular his health condition.

The big question in his mind was if should he find a way to share all the details before the trip and provide her some time to process the information, or wait until they got to Italy and take a chance on ruining their time together. *Well, if you put it that way I should move sooner than later.*

Okay then, now that he made a decision, where and when. Should he ask Sara to come home or would he go to her in the city? He knew he'd want her undivided attention so he guessed at his place would be best. But how would he get her home without making it sound like a life and death matter? He needed a perfect reason that wouldn't alarm her. *Maybe all I need to do is ask. How about just because I miss her and want to spend some time together and let the rest happen naturally.*

No time like the present. He walked to the desk where his phone had been for so many years.

"Good Morning, Mason, Davis, and Milo. How can I help you?" the voice on the other end asked.

"Good morning I would like to speak with Sara Milo please." Jon requested.

"One moment please I will connect you with her executive assistant."

"Good Morning. Attorney Sara Milo's office, may I help you?" Victoria said

"Good Morning Victoria. This is Sara's dad, Jon Milo. May I speak with Sara?"

"Yes, of course, Mr. Milo. I will let her know you are on the phone for her, please hold."

A brief moment passed then Sara came on the line. "Hi Dad, is everything okay? What is going on?" She sounded a bit nervous.

"Hi sweetie, nothing is up except I was wondering if it would be possible for you to come for a visit for a couple of days if you can get away" Jon said, trying his best to sound nonchalant.

"Okay, Dad, now you have me worried. I can't remember the last time you called me and asked me to come home. What's going on?" Sara demanded.

"Well, if you must know I miss you and our time at Christmas was too short and then perhaps I have someone I would like you to meet. Is that okay?" he replied, thinking he would like her to meet Brie soon.

"Wow, Dad, that is nice. Where did you meet her?" Sara asked teasingly.

"I met her on an online dating site that my friend crazy Larry set me up on."

"Dad, have you lost your mind? What the hell are you doing on an online dating site?" Sara said rather loudly. "Don't you know there are all sorts of trolls looking for lonely men with means to take advantage of?" Sara screamed into the phone.

Immediately Sara could hear her father laughing like a little kid. "Honey, I am just pulling your leg. Relax!" Jon told her.

"You'd better be for God's sake, or more importantly your sake," Sara admonished Jon.

"Okay, okay, did you lose your sense of humor recently? Remember, I don't even like being online. I met her at the travel agency I went to for planning our trip, and since then we have had one date. Her name is

Brie, and I think I want to spend more time with her. However, I need your advice on this since I'm out of practice, you might say. Can you make it?" Jon begged.

"Dad that would be wonderful. Hold on a minute, I need to ask Victoria about when I have some space on my calendar. By the way, I may have something to tell you as well." Sara teased.

"Okay, I will wait." Jon agreed.

Putting Dad on hold, Sara thought she'd need to find a way to get even for that stunt. She had to admit to herself he'd had her going. It had been a long time since he tried anything like that and she guessed it was a good sign.

What seemed like a long time passed as Jon waited and he began to think he may have made a mistake putting Brie into the equation but a guy's gotta do what a guy's gotta do. He laughed out loud.

Sara came back on the line. "Dad, Victoria says I can make it two weeks from now and I will make it a long weekend. How about I take the train on Thursday evening, and head back on Sunday?"

"That'd be great," Jon said.

"Oh and Dad, since I'm making the trip I would like to see your plan on how we're working towards improving your kidney functions."

"Sure, honey, we can discuss that if you want to," Jon responded. "I will pick you up at the station, and we will have a great weekend!"

CHAPTER EIGHTEEN

Okay, that was easier than I expected, Jon thought. Sara didn't push for any answers or even ask too many questions. Now he needed to sit down and figure out what he was going to say to her about his past, and his present. The conversation wouldn't be easy. He headed back to his newspaper, still mostly folded on the ottoman.

His coffee was cold and he no longer felt like reading the news. "The hell with the press" he said out loud. "Nothing worthwhile reading as usual."

Peering out the window Jon could see his old beater truck sitting in the driveway. It had served him well for a long time. Maybe it was time to retire the old girl and get something he didn't need to apologize for. His days of needing a truck were over anyway. He could surprise Sara when she arrived on the train. Perhaps something a bit sportier and more likely to be enjoyed by a lady like Brie.

Jon arrived at the Ford dealer about noon. He wasn't sure what to do or what the expectations were but no sooner had he turned off the engine than a salesman came out of the woodwork and approached him. Good grief, Jon thought, this guy was stealthy. Where had he been hiding?

"Good morning sir, how can I help you?" the young salesman asked.

Jon, not wanting to sound too eager, said, "I'm not sure. I am considering trading in my truck."

The salesman looked past Jon at the yellow and rust colored old truck and appeared to do his best to contain a laugh. "Yes, sir, we can make that happen. Do you have anything particular in mind?"

Jon caught the attitude immediately and for a moment was pissed off at the arrogance of this young man, but then realized his truck was older than this fellow so perhaps a laugh was appropriate. He guessed the young man certainly had no appreciation for the quality of the old days at all.

"I need a car that will be reliable, comfortable and hold its value. A bit sporty would be nice too. I have not shopped for a vehicle in a very long time, so I have no idea what you have. I have seen some Mustangs around town, and they look pretty sweet. Are they expensive?" Jon asked innocently.

The young salesman was still doing his best to control his excitement at having a live one but was not doing very well.

Jon noticed this and let him know, "Young man, even though my truck is old as am, don't be fooled by appearances. I am a former Marine, and my daughter is a hotshot attorney in New York. Screw me, and you will have both of us knee-deep in your shit. Got it

"Yes, sir, I do understand," he said, suddenly changing his attitude 180 degrees. "Let us go in the showroom, and I will give you some time to look around, and when you are ready for a test drive of a model you like, then we will do that. How does that sound, sir?" the young man asked politely.

"Good idea young man. By the way, what is your name?" Jon asked.

"My name is Brendan sir," opening the door for Jon.

Jon spent the next half hour opening doors and looking at the stickers of the six different cars in the showroom. *Holy shit, these babies were expensive. This whole idea is crazy. I am not about to spend $45,000.00 to give my sorry old ass a ride. I wonder what my insurance will cost for one of these.*

Jon signaled to Brendan to come over and as the young man approached Jon asked. "Do you also sell used cars? Something that is two or three years old and more reasonable?"

Brendan shook his head and replied, "Yes sir, of course we do. Do you have a specific model in mind?"

"Not really but as I said more reasonable." Jon repeated. "Young man, you should know that I am not used to repeating myself."

Brendan got the message, but his rebuttal was that financing was available for longer terms than in the past and the payments could be suited to Jon's needs.

"Son, I have no interest in making payments on anything. If I can't pay cash for it, I don't buy it. Besides, at my age do you honestly think I want to commit to a long-term payment plan? That would be pretty stupid and I assure you I am not stupid," Jon let him know.

"Yes, sir," Brendan said as they made their way to the door towards the used car lot.

While they walked out to the lot, Jon was able to observe this young man. His gait told Jon that he indeed did not have any military experience. He couldn't have even been in the Army. Even the Army had some marching skills and characteristics. His manner of dress was less than what he thought was a professional look what with his shirt outside the pants, loafers, no socks and no tie. The look spoke volumes. The real kicker was the haircut. He had some ball of hair posted atop his head like an enormous bird had flown over and made a deposit and so much grease in it that it was shiny. Again, no military history there whatsoever. Jon laughed to himself, realizing he was a dinosaur. He did give the young man credit for manners once he stopped laughing at his old beater.

Jon got back to his house late in the day, driving his new wheels. He had found an SUV that would suit him very well. It was spotless, only two years old, with low mileage. He reasoned that an SUV was not a car and not a truck, classy and comfortable enough for a lady and would be useful in the winters of the northeast. He wasn't sure why a moon roof was such a big deal, but it was something he thought that Brie would perhaps like on a beautiful day or evening.

Jon realized he'd already made a lot of plans and assumptions about a lady with whom he'd only enjoyed one date. Had he lost his mind? He was pretty sure Sara would appreciate his upgrade though. It sure smelled better at least, it was quiet, and air conditioning worked. Living large as they said.

CHAPTER NINETEEN

Sara decided that it was time to touch base with Mr. Roselli again and perhaps let him know what she was doing about the recognition for Dad. Sara dialed the phone. She didn't have a lot to tell him but did want to get some more background on their relationship and what he remembered.

"Hello, Roselli here." The voice sounded slightly perturbed.

"Good Morning, Mr. Roselli, this is Sara Milo."

"Good morning, Sara, I am delighted to hear from you. How are you and the Sarge doing?"

"I am well," Sara shared, "and Dad is doing pretty well also. I wanted to let you know I have filed the papers, and I have a Congressman working with me to get it through the proper channels, but I don't have any news about that as yet."

"I figured it was going to be quite a challenge," Roselli said, his voice now kind and sincere. "I am so glad you are doing this."

"Me too. Mr. Roselli, I need to ask, since you're not that far away. Why have you not tried to contact Dad and get together?"

"Sara, a few years back I tried to connect with him on multiple occasions, and he simply chose not to respond. I did get his phone number and address. I called and left a couple of messages and also sent him a letter. I never heard back from him. I really don't know why. Do you? Has he ever mentioned me?" Roselli asked earnestly.

"Mr. Roselli, I am pretty sure the reason he never responded is that Dad doesn't actually *know* what happened to him that night in the jungle when he was wounded. If he does, he has never shared the memory with me. I don't know if he just chose to block it out all these years or something else is going on. I think it's something Dad has had to deal with for a very long time." Sara explained.

"That is all entirely possible. I have talked with many veterans, and that's the case a lot of them. I work as a volunteer at the VA, and in my discussions with some vets who went through situations like your father; it is more common than we might think. I consider myself lucky in some ways and unlucky in others. My memory is very clear of that night, and there are times I wish it weren't. So I understand the battle your Dad has been fighting, I can only hope to help him." Roselli offered.

Sara asked, "By any chance do you have any photos from those days that I could use to help Dad's memory if he wants help?"

"Yes, I do," Roselli responded. "I have a few of our old outfit, and I can have some copies made and mail them to you. Please be careful showing them to the Sarge. I am sure you know him best and can choose the right time."

"I understand. Listen, if it all works out, would you be willing to visit us and get reacquainted with Dad?" Sara asked.

"Yes, of course, let's not forget I owe the Sarge my life and I will do anything to help," Roselli promised.

"Thank you, Mr. Roselli, I will be in touch. I'll watch for your photos and I really want to thank you."

"Goodbye, Sara and be well. Take good care of the Sarge for all of us."

Hanging up the phone, Sara understood that this would be a very complicated situation. She might need some help but she couldn't believe that the past left in the past would be good for Dad, or anyone.

Right when Sara hung up the phone, Victoria knocked on the door and entered. "Boss, we have some news. The police are here and would like to speak with you and the name partners in the conference room."

Entering the conference room Sara walked over and stood next to Mr. Mason and Mr. Davis. Once they were seated, the receptionist brought in the NYPD Captain of Detectives. Captain Wilson was tall and by most standards a handsome but rough looking man. Well dressed and all business his sharp eyes and satisfied smile put Sara at ease but she also knew without a doubt this was a man who could handle himself in almost any situation; he exuded confidence.

"Ms. Milo, Mr. Mason, and Mr. Davis, I have news for you, and I am sure you will consider it all good. As you know, we have been investigating the accident of your associate Mr. Evans since Christmas. Shortly after the crash, we had reason to believe that foul play was involved. We had sources that led us to believe that Mr. Evans was involved with some people of suspicious activities and these activities led to the need for the removal of Mr. Evans.

"We can now tell you, beyond a shadow of a doubt, the Mr. Evans in our information is a different Evans and not your associate. I am not able to provide details from the investigation. However, we have concluded that the death of your Mr. Evans was a regrettable and utterly unconnected accident. We are sorry for the confusion and concern, but we did want to be sure as always," the Captain explained.

Mr. Mason thanked the Captain for his resolve in this delicate matter. We appreciate you coming to tell us the truth so quickly."

After the Police had left the room, there was a very definite air of relief, not only that their dear friend and colleague was not in the wrong, but that the firm's reputation was intact and that Mrs. Evans would not suffer through anything more.

Sara went back to her office on a high and motioned Vic into her office.

"Victoria, please see if you can locate Congressman Platt. I want to make sure he knows the news." directed Sara.

"Yes ma'am," replied Victoria with a huge smile.

The phone buzzed, and Sara grabbed the receiver. "Devon, hello, I am so sorry to bother you, but I have some great news," she said excitedly.

"Sara, you are not a bother. It's so good to hear from you. What's the great news?" asked Devon.

"The police were just here and informed us the investigation cleared Mr. Evans and our firm. The information they had was regarding a different man named Evans, so it's over."

"That is outstanding," Devon responded. "I am sure you are all relieved. I didn't believe any of it for a minute. "

"I didn't either, but it wouldn't be the first time I was surprised. I am very grateful it is all over. How are you? I have often thought about our evening together and would like a repeat if you would," Sara said with a smile in her voice. "I should also say that I could really get used to riding on your motorcycle which I suspect is even more fun in warm weather."

"I was thinking the same thing and have been for a while. Sadly, I am stuck here in DC for a while yet. We have some legislation coming up that I need to be around for to make my involvement clear. What would you think about coming to Washington for a weekend?" Devon asked.

Sara was shocked at the question but undoubtedly thrilled as well. "I might be able to make that work. I have to go to Massachusetts first for a weekend with my Dad. It was his idea, and that's unusual, so I suspect it is important to him." Sara explained.

"I understand for sure. Perhaps after that, we can make some time to get to know each other. I have spare bedrooms in my home here, so no pressure of any kind." Devon said

Sara chuckled to herself. *If you only knew what is going through my mind.* But if it made him more comfortable then that was good by her.

"Devon, I still think back to our day on your bike. It was amazing and I want to do that again. Of course I will need to do some shopping for next time. About coming to Washington, the train from the City is an easy trip. We will make it happen as soon as possible!"

"Thank you, Sara, and I look forward to making plans as soon as you are available. Bye for now."

Hanging up the phone, Sara realized she had a lot of feelings jumping around in her mind and a certain tingle in her stomach that made her feel like a schoolgirl. She loved talking to him, loved the sound of his voice. She felt like she was walking a tightrope with Dad and Devon each pulling at her and it was her job to stay in balance.

No doubt in her mind that Dad would have to come first. She suspected it was time for a confrontation about his lack of willingness to improve his health. Perhaps he didn't believe he had the power to do anything or he was just uncomfortable with change which was probably a large part of the problem, considering how little had changed in his life all of these years including his damn truck.

It was also time to get the answers to so many questions she'd had all of these years. Feeling a bit selfish she knew she needed the answers, not just wanted them. *I want to know all of him and not just the wonderful man that was so good to me growing up. His strength is incredible, and I hope I can find some for myself.*

How did he happen to go to Viet Nam in the first place? She knew of the draft of that time, but she was quite sure he had not been drafted and chose to join the Marine Corps on his own. What led him to do that? Did his parents push him in that direction or did he make his own choices? Sara had an excellent education, so she knew the times were different for him than for her but what had molded him to be the man he was and how did he become the man he was today? What were his influences? She also had a real hunger to know more about her Mother.

Good grief, she thought, *the poor guy is going to be overwhelmed. Can I expect answers to all of this? Somehow I suspect Dad wants to give me these answers and maybe more soon. I feel he is finally ready to let me in like never before. I sure hope so as I love this man so very much. He is my hero no matter what happens with the government.* Sara recalled how often her mother had kept her from being nosy with her dad and how she protected him about those days in his life and as she got older she respected that so much.

Arriving back to her apartment Sara sat down with a glass of her favorite Bordeaux and put her feet up. The view from her apartment was terrific, and she sat there in the dark, letting the lights from the most incredible city in the world fill the room. A lot had happened today with the mystery of Mr. Evans being cleared up, her conversation with Devon and most importantly her Dad's request for her to visit.

It was days like this that she was so appreciative of having Victoria handle so much of her work. Preparing the contracts, managing the associates who did the research and so much more; without her, she would have no time for anything. She needed to do something special for Vic.

CHAPTER TWENTY

I t was Wednesday, and Jon had an appointment with his Doc at the VA. More test results were back, and it was truth time. On the way to the VA in his new SUV Jon was feeling pretty good about things in general. Sara would be visiting in a couple of days and his last conversation with Brie sounded promising in several ways. He had finally come out of the dark ages and bought a new vehicle. He realized that it was so quiet riding in his new mode of transportation he could enjoy listening to the radio as he drove. He laughed at himself.

Of course, the downside was that his financial net worth had taken a hit. Not a severe one but a hit nonetheless. He was in fact quite proud of himself as he believed he had worked a great deal from the young car salesman. Of course, there was the possibility that the kid let him think that. But either way, Jon was happy with the dea. And to top it all off the inside of his new

Explorer didn't stink. That was a noticeable change and benefit for sure.

Arriving at the clinic a bit early for his appointment was normal for Jon. He often admitted that his penchant for being on time was just who he was and at the VA that had often proven to be a good thing. Sometimes the Vet who had an appointment in front of him was a no-show, and he would get called in early. He couldn't understand why someone would be a no-show and not call to cancel their appointment. That was just disrespectful in his book. According to one of the staff he chatted with some time ago, more than half of the appointments made by Vets were not kept. No wonder there was such a backlog.

Sitting in the waiting room often gave Jon some time to think about what he needed to do in the coming days and weeks, and today his thoughts were all about Sara. He had decided that no matter what the doc said he would share with Sara all the details. She had a right to know. If the news were less than pleasant, she would need some time to process and deal with whatever. He was quite confident that they would handle it together, as usual.

The affable and energetic nurse came through the door and called him by name. Acknowledging her from across the waiting room, Jon followed her through the door and into the examining room where the Navy

Commander was already waiting. Shaking hands, Jon felt like he should salute but that would not be appropriate since he was out of uniform and indoors. Marines didn't salute indoors and uncovered (not wearing a hat).

"Good morning Sir," Jon said.

"Good morning Sergeant, how have you been?" asked the Commander.

"Well sir, I'm doing just fine as best I can tell. I even broke down and bought a new vehicle for the first time in many years." Jon said proudly.

"Good for you, Sergeant." responded the Commander. "So, I have your test results here, and I think we need to discuss them without delay. There is no way to ease into this kind of information. Jon, you are really at risk, and the issues do not have a easy solution for the most part. I am sorry to tell you, but your kidneys are failing. You have progressed to stage three kidney disease, and at stage five you will need a transplant and certainly dialysis."

"The agent orange is taking its toll with your diabetes, and that is affecting your kidneys very negatively. The meds you are on are slowing the progression but will not delay it indefinitely and will not cure the disease," the Doc explained.

Jon sat in stunned silence. He had no idea what to say or what questions to ask. His first thoughts, of course, went to Sara and how she would handle the news. For himself, his mind went to the fact he had just bought a new car.

"Ok Doc, what kind of time are we talking about and is there anything I can do to slow the progression? Also, what about a transplant? Is that even feasible at my age?"

"Sergeant you can slow it down for sure with a better diet and regular exercise, but I have concerns that you can make these changes in your life since you haven't made them already.

Jon thought he sounded a little like Sara.

"Regarding a transplant, that will be difficult because of your age and other health factors such as your diabetes and high blood pressure. I am confident we can manage your discomfort that will eventually come. My best-educated guess on time is about two years before you will notice any changes or additional symptoms but I have to let you know it is coming based on what we know today. How fast it happens does depend on you somewhat. Your diet is about the best defense you have. I can provide you a lot of information on that, and the VA offers some classes on nutrition that you should attend. Also, Jon, if you remember I asked you to keep a chart for your blood pressure. Did you do that?"

"Yes I did, and I remembered to bring it with me," Jon said proudly, handing the doc the sheet of paper.

Jon sat silently while the Dr. looked over the chart. He seemed to take a longer time than necessary, which alerted Jon a bit.

"Jon by the looks of this chart and the numbers spiking we have a situation that would appear to be dangerous. Your blood pressure fluctuates. Low in the morning and after a day of regular activity it is showing higher than I am comfortable with. I want to schedule you for an angiogram and see what is happening with your main arteries and heart valves. I am concerned about blockages. Would you agree with my plan?"

"Yes Sir doc, if you think it's necessary," Jon said.

"It is. Do you have any other questions?"

"Yeah Doc, how do I tell my daughter?" Jon asked rhetorically.

On the drive home Jon rolled the news around in his mind. He was still in a bit of shock but if he were being honest with himself he knew it was coming. Now that the time had arrived it certainly did not make the news any easier to swallow. He was indeed not afraid of dying but he felt he still had so much more living to do. He finally committed in his mind to diet change and exercise that he had been ignoring, if only to delay the inevitable long enough to accomplish some particular things.

He realized that honesty with those he cared about would have to be paramount. He certainly could not ask Brie to be involved with him and not know what was going on. That would not be fair. Regarding Sara, he would tell her all and hope like crazy to make their time together count in many ways.

The difficulty in accepting the diagnosis was that at the moment he did not feel sick. No symptoms in his mind equated to feeling just fine with nothing to worry about. He decided that he would need to do some research to find out what he could expect as evidence of changes to his health.

On the way home, he suddenly realized he had headed towards the travel agency and found himself pulling into a parking spot. Staring at the building he tried to decide whether to go in and see if Brie could get away for lunch. He questioned whether or not he should tell her in the middle of the day or wait to make a date to see her one evening this week. The powerful need to tell someone was overpowering and Jon had no one else with which to share the bad news. Briefly, he thought maybe he could call some of the guys he worked with for years, but out of the blue to reach out to share this personal news did not make any sense nor was it anyone's business, except his and those he was close to.

Shutting down the car Jon went into the office. He could see Brie was on the phone so he took a seat and waited for her to finish. Jon thought about what he would say and how he would say it, but his biggest concern was ruining her day halfway through. Maybe he would ask her to dinner and then tell her in private to give her time to think and deal with her emotions if she had some for him. Somehow he would have to make it clear that he did not want to be mothered or smothered, that whatever time they had together would be a gift and pleasurable. Perhaps even knowing that time was limited would help them make the best of it without regrets.

A moment later Brie walked over to Jon, and when he stood, she hugged him right in front of everyone. *Wow,* he thought, *this is wonderful.*

"Well hello," he said, "Thanks for that wonderful greeting."

" Jon, if we were alone my greeting would still be happening," she said with a beautiful smile on her pretty face. "What are you doing here anyway?"

"Well, I stopped by to see if you were available for dinner tonight," Jon said, looking into her incredible eyes.

"Well, I did have big plans to go home and make myself dinner tonight and spend the evening sitting in front of the TV, since a certain man had not reached out to me. So to answer your question, yes I am available, and in fact, I want to cook for you tonight at my house if that's okay?"

Jon flashed a sheepish smile. "I know I haven't called for a few days, and I am sorry. I was trying not to be pushy. Yes, I would love to dine with you tonight. May I bring some wine? Anything else I can bring and what time?" Jon fired off the questions.

"Well good looking, 6 p.m. would be just about perfect as long as you don't mind watching me cook and talking at the same time. If you do, seven would be the right time to eat." Brie reached out to take his hand in hers.

Jon smiled broadly and said, "Six will be just perfect."

He left the office feeling light on his feet and excited to spend time with Brie again. Trying to stay under control until she knew the score would not be easy. She was a fantastic woman to be around. Her energy reminded him of his late wife, and her body was equally as beautiful. He wished she had come into his life years ago.

At precisely six Jon pulled into the driveway of Brie's lovely home. Getting out of the car he saw Brie standing at the entrance with a look of surprise on her face.

"Okay, new car and you didn't tell me why?" She asked.

"Well I was planning on surprising you on our date. After all, it's your fault I bought it," he said with sincerity.

"My fault, really? And how is that my fault?" she challenged with a smile.

"Well, when I first met you I couldn't figure out how to take you out and ask you to ride in that old beater truck of mine. Certainly not something a lady like yourself should be riding in, or be seen in for that matter. So based on that I bought it, and that is how it is your fault. At least in my mind." Jon said, smirking.

"Hmmm…I wasn't the one that made you keep that old hunk of a truck for so many years. So accept that it was time, no matter whether you met me or not," Brie said with a laugh. "Now get your butt inside, it's cold out here."

Brie's home was so inviting and comfortable, and once his jacket was hung up on the hat tree next to the door, Jon went into the kitchen in search of a corkscrew. He located it quickly, opened the wine and poured it into the decanter to let it breathe for a while before dining.

He decided that putting off the bad news would not make it easier for either of them, so getting on with it was the best thing to do.

"Brie, Can we sit down for a moment? I have something to tell you."

"Of course," she said as she led him to the couch in the living room. They sat in front of the fireplace, glowing with a warmth that added to the ambiance of the home.

"Brie, we have been friends for only a short time but in that time I have discovered feelings that I thought I would never experience again, and I do get a sense that you have feelings for me too. Now, what I don't know is if all you want is my body or my heart. In my case I can assure you my heart has more value than my body," he said, trying to make light of what was coming. "I am not expecting an answer as yet, but I feel I owe you the truth no matter where it may or may not lead."

"Jon, my feelings about you are genuine to me. I want to get to know you in every way. It has been a very long time for me as well you know, but I feel close to you and am intrigued by you at the same time. I want to know more, much more. Does that answer your question?"

"Sort of, yes. And it sounds terrific, but before we get too involved, I need you to know some specifics." He took a deep breath and continued. "I went to the VA today, and at my Dr.'s conference, I received some information that is indeed not great news. As you know, I have diabetes and other issues from my exposure to Agent Orange in Viet Nam so long ago.

"Adding to that is the big problem of kidney disease. My kidneys are failing and in a couple of years, assuming that the progression is the same as in recent past, I will be needing a transplant or at a minimum, dialysis. I also have high blood pressure that is somewhat under control but not improving enough. I am telling you all of this for two reasons. One I needed to tell someone, and you were the only person besides Sara I am close enough with to share.

"Second, I want a relationship with you but the expectations of this relationship need to be understood so you know up front what I can offer and what I can't and the only can't is anything long term. I want to spend as much time with you as possible and to have that time be unique, but I do not want to be mothered or smothered and treated any differently. If you can handle that, then I am yours for as long as I am here," Jon finished.

Brie sat in silence for what seemed like forever. She got up and walked into the kitchen and took out the steaks, poured them both some wine from the decanter and walked back into the living room, still in silence. After putting down the wine on the coffee table in front of them, Brie reached out and moved Jon's arms out of the way and climbed into his lap, putting her head on his shoulder snuggling so close, still in silence.

They sat there listening to the fire crackle and to each other breathing. The words would not come to either of them, not that Jon had anything left to say. All he could do was give her the time she needed to process this news and his requirements and wait for her to speak. Her climbing into his lap spoke volumes, but he remained quiet.

Finally, Brie picked up her head from his shoulder put a hand on each side of his face and brought her beautiful red lips to his. Slowly ending the kiss, Brie said all that was necessary. "I am in for the duration if you will have me." Tears slid down her soft cheeks and her blue eyes filled with more tears to follow.

Jon responded by pulling her tight into his arms, and together they shed tears of mixed emotions. He thought to himself, *this is the last time we dwell on this. Now is the time for living and not for dying.*

Jon, desperate to change the subject decided to broach the topic of the letter on the mantle from the Marine Corp. "Brie, the first time I was here I couldn't help but notice the framed letter with the Marine Corps emblem on it. At the time I didn't have my glasses on so I couldn't read it. I am curious what that's about."

Brie smiled at him. Walking over to the mantle she took the frame and brought it to Jon. "It's not really a big deal. A couple years ago some of my co-workers and myself volunteered during the holidays for the Toys for Tots Campaign, which is sponsored by the Marine Corps. The local reserve unit thanked us with this." She handed Jon the picture frame.

"Very nice and well deserved," Jon said, chuckling. "I had been wondering and thought maybe you were a Marine in your past life. This is much better."

After a quiet but delicious dinner and some other non-medical discussions, Jon went home to get some sleep in preparation for Sara's arrival the next day. Drifting off to sleep he thought genuinely about how he would tell her his "news," and he had serious concerns as to how she would handle the situation. He knew she was tough and Sara had known for some time that he had serious health issues. Perhaps she wouldn't be all that surprised. "Time for lights out," he said aloud as he reached for the switch on the old lamp that had been by his bed for way too many years.

CHAPTER
TWENTY ONE

I t was a miserably hot morning for Jon and his company of Marines. Last night was uneventful; they had the night off. Typically that meant the next day whatever came down from above was going to be theirs Jon thought as he headed down the muddy trail to the company HQ for a meeting with his platoon commander and his company commander.

He knew he had a new 2nd Lieutenant coming in and did not have any information as yet about him. Before Jon left his area, he made sure the platoon was out of their racks and getting their gear squared away for whatever might be coming at them. What they all wouldn't give for just a few minutes in some cool air conditioning. On his last trip to the Da Nang Air Force Base, he couldn't help but notice their Quonset huts had

A/C units sticking out of the walls. *Guess I should have joined the Air Force,* he laughed.

Opening the door to the CO's tent, Jon was greeted by the Major and told to find a seat. The briefing started out as usual with the orders of the day, and then the Major began to explain an assignment the unit had been given. It was far from ordinary.

"A unit from 3rd Battalion was attacked hard last night, and they need some support for tonight, and we are going to provide it. Our assignment is to fill in the positions that are now unmanned and to also man a couple of tanks. The men in those tanks have not slept in two days and need some relief. The force will consist of 1st platoon along with two squads from the weapons platoon. The remainder of the company will stay on alert and be ready to travel if needed. The platoon will assemble at 1400 with all field gear, including full loads of ammo and grenades. Trucks will take the platoon to the landing zone to board choppers to be dropped off at the LZ near the camp. The LZ is outside the wire so be sure to set a perimeter as you get on the ground." Major Watson ordered.

The Major continued, "Each of you Non-Coms needs to make sure your men have all of the gear in perfect condition, and their minds are clear. This will not be an easy mission, and you should expect enemy activity in the wee hours as usual. Watch your asses in the

LZ. It is always possible Charlie will have something to greet you with. Your grateful hosts will provide cover fire for your landing, but the first chopper in should be sure to set an LZ perimeter for the following birds. You will take all orders from the camp Commander and assist in whatever way he feels best. Is that clear?"

"Any questions, men?"

Soon after they were dismissed.

"Lieutenant Kao I want you to meet Sergeant Milo. He is your platoon Sergeant and has experience and solid knowledge of this shithole," the Major said in all seriousness.

Lieutenant Kao walked forward and extended his hand to Jon. "Pleased to meet you, sergeant," the butter bar said, looking Jon squarely in his eyes.

"Same here," Jon responded. "Welcome aboard, sir."

The Major looked at Jon and told him, "That will be all Sergeant."

"Aye-aye, Sir," Jon said. He did his usual about face and left the tent.

After Jon was gone the Major turned to the new 2nd Lt., and with an intense and penetrating look told him in no uncertain terms, "Lt. you are so new here it is frightening, but you have gotten lucky in one respect. You are taking over a platoon that happens to have one of the best Non-Coms around, and while I can't order you to take his advice on just about everything, you would be wise to do so. If you do, you may live long enough to learn much of what he knows, and that will get you home again. He knows his men inside and out, their strengths and their weaknesses and he will handle them accordingly. His ability to stay calm in dangerous situations is a talent that few men have, so watch and learn. Do you get my message?"

"Yes, sir I certainly do, and I appreciate the advice." the young lieutenant answered.

"Very good. Be sure your men are ready at 1400 hrs and do an equipment check with your platoon. By the way, the CO in the unit you are supporting is a Captain Lewis and is very experienced. Follow his direction to the letter," the Major ordered.

"Aye-aye Sir," the lieutenant responded and turned and left the tent.

When Jon returned to his platoon area, he called a meeting with the squad leaders to fill them in on the assignment. He reminded each to make sure the gear was all ready to go, and each man had his supply of salt pills. "The heat will be miserable, and we don't want men passing out," Jon said.

Getting his own gear together, Jon came to the realization that this would be the first helicopter insertion for most of the men. He knew first-hand the adrenaline rush that they would experience. The sound of the rotors would be deafening and the take off and landing would have its own attack on their senses.

When they got the signal for landing each man would have different degrees of fear in the unknown, the unknown being if the LZ was hot or not, meaning under fire or threat of attack. Also the terrain could be anything from raw dirt to six feet of elephant grass. In either case the choppers most likely would not touch the ground and each man would be required to jump the last number of feet, depending on how generous the pilot was. His hope was that each of the men would remember their training and move away from the drop spot and get into a defensive perimeter position to provide cover for the following helicopters.

Because they were going in to an established base-camp it was most likely to be a cool LZ but the anticipation was always the same. John knew the same old fears of screwing up was on each man's mind, including his own.

Jon knew he needed to watch each man closely, particularly the new guys, to make sure they unloaded their weapons getting in and loaded them before they get out. Making sure each put the safe on so the jump to the ground wouldn't cause an accidental firing and put a hole in the chopper or in the man next to him.

The rotor wash threw up dust and debris, making movement difficult and only hand signals worked with the noise of the chopper. Jon felt a reasonable amount of confidence in his men based on past experiences but nonetheless he knew he had to be on his toes and keep his head on a swivel.

At 1355 the platoon was in loose formation and every man was ready to move out. The trucks arrived, and Jon got them loaded into the 6x6's for the short ride to the helicopters LZ. Each chopper could carry twelve men with gear so there would be five choppers in total; re-supply material for the camp would take some of the available space. The force consisted of precisely 56 Marines and their equipment.

The only gear they needed was weapons and personal items such as the all-important toilet paper. Could never have too much of that and the bug juice, the essential bug juice. As far as they knew the assignment was only for 48 hours from touchdown. C-Rats were already at the camp along with water.

The landing went off without a hitch for all the men and equipment. Jon was glad the jungle was not thick and close. He signaled the men into a tight perimeter, facing them out away from the LZ to watch for any enemy snipers or an ambush. Once all the men had been inserted, Jon led them towards the wire, making sure they had a rear guard. As he approached the camp, he was able to see Marines inside covering their movement towards the camp.

Jon stood just inside the wire and did a head count as the Marines living here full time closed the hole in the wire. Cpt. Lewis approached the Lt. and had a conversation that Jon could not hear. Jon suddenly realized that on the whole trip the Lt. was quiet and never said a word. Nothing better he thought that a new Lt. that knew his place.

A few minutes later Lt. Kao came to Jon with an outline of what they were being asked to do. "Fill in the vacant spots and give these men a chance to sleep as soon as possible."

In the middle of the camp was one huge tank. The Lt. suggested that Jon take that turret as his spot and from there he would be able to see the whole camp in case of an attack. The tank had a starlight scope on the turret for viewing the terrain in front of the camp after dark. The Lt. said he would stay with the heavy weapons squad and would take direction from Jon in the tank. The tank was equipped with a field telephone with a direct line to the CO's hooch.

Jon thought to himself, *what the fuck do I know about a tank? Hope the guys that run this thing can get me up to speed fast.*

Daylight faded quickly, and as the night fell over the camp, Jon was sitting in the tank turret. Looking through the starlight scope, he could see small campfires off in the distance which no doubt was Charlie, cooking rice. Rotating the turret from side to side gave him an unusual view of the whole area in front of them. Could those little bastards believe they had a chance against his Marines in this well-fortified position? Of course they did, and if there were enough of them, they could kick ass. *Here I sit thanks to some stupid and safe politicians*, he thought.

Damn it was dark tonight, clouds hiding all the stars as usual. Jon was also aware how quiet it was. Anywhere else in the world the quiet would be welcome. Here it scared the hell out of all of them. Just then he realized one of the guys down in the bowels of the tank had started to snore, and he found it somehow reassuring and laughable.

Jon sat there in the dark being very vigilant with his scope and fighting the urge to sleep. The other two guys in the tank were fast asleep as evidenced by the snoring duet now. The waiting was the toughest part, he thought to himself, but then knew that was not true. The thinking was hard not to do, and it did happen every night. Thinking about back home and family. Assuming that he only had about six months left in this hellhole. Asking himself why they were even there was a habit that was taking on a life of its own.

In early 1965 not much was known about Viet Nam and being the first Marines in, minimal experience or preparation was available. The propaganda given was that they were here to stop the spread of communism. As best as he could tell they should let the communists have this dump; too damn hot and too wet.

It was about 2 a.m., and on his last turn with the turret scope, he was sure he saw movement about 200 yards in front. Moving back to the spot he waited, and while he watched he looked at the distance gauge on the screen. He was right. He could see men crawling and low walking through the weeds and brush towards the wire. Grabbing the field telephone, he cranked the handle to raise the operator in the HQ. Whispering just loud enough to be heard, Jon said, "This is Milo in Tank position one. I have movement 100 yards directly in front approaching the wire."

Reaching for his M-14, he woke up the two tank men and showed them what he was seeing. Climbing down from the tank, Jon headed for one of the positions near the center of the line near the wire. He wanted to be close to his men and make sure they did their job. The night was so quiet. The only sounds to be heard were coming from the night animals off in the jungle. That was unless he counted the sounds of men breathing deep and doing their level best to remain quiet. Jon knew the whole camp was at the ready and once the flares went up from their mortars, all hell would break loose. Rifles, machine guns, recoilless rifles and even a tank might have its say. Those sneaky bastards out in front had no idea how pissed off these Marines were.

Jon checked his magazine on his M-14 and clicked off the safety. Just then the whoosh of a mortar flare sounded overhead from the center of the compound and lit up the entire field of fire. At that moment red tracers began flying into the camp, and green tracers went out to meet them. The main line opened up, and body after body could be seen falling face down and not moving. The sound of incoming mortars was unmistakable, and as they landed, it was clear Charlie had the camp zeroed in.

Fortunately, they had zeroed in on the positions from the night before, and the CO knew better than to put his Marines in the same areas. The noise was incredible and could make a man's teeth shake, but the outgoing ordinance was too much for the black pajama night crawlers, and the whole battle lasted only about fifteen minutes, according to Jon's watch. It sure seemed like a lot longer, but it ended as quickly as it started.

Jon couldn't help wonder what the hell Charlie hoped to gain with that. The whole attack made no tactical sense, at least not yet.

The sun came up just about as hot as it had gone down and those that had been able to get back to sleep a few hours ago were climbing out of their holes and heading to the appropriate area to utilize some of that so important paper they had brought. One thing about C Rations, men went regularly, and no doubt the water that tasted like jet fuel from the used fuel tanks contributed to bodily functions. Between the heat, poor quality water, and lousy tasting food most Marines lost a lot of weight in the Nam and those that got the malaria lost plenty more.

The nagging thought that they were there for no reason was always close at hand. *Hell, even the Vietnamese people didn't want us here. They're tired of war, and so are we.* It was getting harder and harder to hold on to the belief that he was making a difference. Somehow, someone was making money from this fiasco, and he was quite sure it wasn't him or his men. That left the politicians. As he thought of the word politician, he recalled a comment he had heard some time ago. Diapers and politicians need to be changed regularly and most often for the same reason. If only he could see the humor, but he was not in the mood.

The word soon came down that his platoon was heading out and back to their area. The balance of the command here would also be leaving within a short time. It had apparently been determined by the top brass that nothing was being solved holding this place and assets being used here were needed elsewhere. When the word spread, there was a mild celebration, and most likely if these men hadn't been so exhausted from the heat, lack of sleep and overwhelming fear, there might have been an even bigger party.

The lieutenant came to Jon and asked him to get the men ready to leave. The choppers would start coming in about 1100, and they would have to be prepared to get on board quickly and smoothly.

"Aye-aye sir," Jon replied

Calling his four squad leaders together his instructions for the departure were clear. Each squad would take a chopper one at a time to leave the wire. The host Marines of the camp would provide the perimeter for the choppers to make it quicker to load and get away. He reminded them that they needed to be sure to keep the men low on the ground as the aircrafts land. Be sure to unload all weapons getting onboard. Jon would be in the last chopper as was his choice. The Lt. should be in the first one to be in command in the air.

One by one they came and picked up the men. As Jon ran towards his chopper, he heard gunfire. The helicopter was taking fire. Seeing the tracers coming from the jungle Jon waved off the pilot and headed back to the camp in a low crawl. The chopper made a getaway without damage, but now Jon was on his own, lying in the grass unsure where to shoot if anywhere.

Lying there as still as possible he listened to his surroundings, trying to get an idea of what to do next. All of a sudden six men came running by him, headed in the direction the tracers came from. Jon thought to himself, *what the hell, better than lying here in the dirt.* Jumping up he followed the patrol. When they reached the hidden area that they believed the shooting came from they were already gone. Typical Cong tactic.

"Hit and run, and boy can they disappear fast and no noise either," said one of the men. Jon and his new team made their way back to the base camp. Captain Lewis approached Jon. "Sergeant Milo, I suspect you saved a lot of lives when you waved off that pilot and hit the dirt." the Captain said, slapping him on his helmet.

"Well Sir, I don't think I had much choice. Besides, I knew your men were close by," Jon said, wiping the sweat and dirt from his face. "Sir, any idea when I will be able to get back to my unit?" Jon asked.

"Sergeant, I will do my best to get you a ride on the first chopper that comes in. Thanks again Marine," the cool officer said as he headed to his hooch.

Jon opened his eyes and knew that same old damn movie was playing in his head once more. *Would these damn dreams ever stop? How the hell can a dream play over and over and never change? What does that mean?* he asked himself. *Maybe one day I will have some answers. For now, I need to shit, shower and shave. Sara will be here this morning and well, it is going to be a day. Good or bad, no idea yet.*

CHAPTER TWENTY-TWO

Sara woke early on Wednesday morning, knowing she had a full day and would be leaving the next morning to spend a long weekend with Dad. She had been dying to know what was going on but knew him well enough not to push for answers that he would deliver in his own time and his way. In all honesty, Sara had much to talk with him about also. She couldn't help wonder how on earth to broach the subject of Roselli and whether she should tell him about their efforts to get him the recognition he deserved. Sara had questions about her childhood and her memories of him back then. Was this the right time or was this just an opportunity to meet his new friend? Could she be more than a friend so soon? That would be the best thing ever, she thought.

She had decided to take the train to avoid traffic and car rental idiots. The train always provided an opportunity to relax for a while and unwind from her high-pressure existence.

The train conductor, who had most likely been doing the same thing every day for many years, walked up the aisle announcing the arrival to Sara's destination. Looking out the window, she just happened to see Dad pacing about the platform. She looked on in amazement, thinking that pacing was so unlike him. He must really be nervous about her coming to visit. Reaching for her bag in the compartment above her seat she thought it had to be one or the other of two things. His love life or his health. There was a chance it was both. Sara reminded herself not to panic in either situation and to be as supportive as possible.

Climbing down the steps to the platform she saw that her father hadn't spotted her yet. Walking towards him with the sounds of her high-heeled boots and the wheels of her luggage clacking over the wooden platform planks she made quite an entrance. Perhaps it was this noise that caused Jon to whirl around and face her as she approached.

Spotting her quickly Jon broke into a wide grin and put his arms out to greet her just like he often did when she was coming home from school as a little girl. Sara saw those widespread arms and instantly felt like a little girl once more. *No matter how old I get this will always be the best feeling in the world.*

"Hi sweetie, so glad you could make it. Welcome home," Jon gushed as he circled his arms tightly around her.

Sara dropped the handle on her suitcase and threw both arms around her dad's neck and squeezed. "Hi Dad, I am so happy to be home with you. How are you?" she asked.

The embrace lasted for a few moments, and no words were spoken. It was just a moment that both were grateful for and a moment to be enjoyed and stored away in their collective memory banks.

Breaking the embrace, Jon finally said, "I'm good. Let's go, I have a great weekend planned." He beamed, taking her hand and her luggage handle.

Sara looked at her father and said "Oh really, and what is so special? I thought this was just a relaxing week-end together." She knew full well it was much more.

"Yes, of course, it is, but I have a few things to share with my daughter as well. Like…we have a new ride waiting," John said, pointing to his new SUV.

"Dad! You finally parted with that old truck after all of these years. What brought this about, or should I ask who?" Sara said with a mischievous grin.

"To be honest, her name is Brie, but she is not the only reason," he said defensively.

"Dad, whatever the reason I am proud of you for making the decision. Tell me more about Brie, please." Sara begged.

"I will honey, but let's get home and relax first. I have much to tell you about a lot of things," Jon said softly.

The ride home was unusually quiet for the occasion, but Sara knew better than to press her father. Pulling in the driveway, Sara thought that not much else had changed as far as she could tell. Opening the front door, she was aware that everything looked the same except neater and even cleaner.

Clearly, Dad was trying to impress someone. Sara took her suitcase to her room and decided to change into more comfortable shoes first and then see what was on Dad's agenda.

Walking into the living room, Jon was already in his favorite chair and had a tray of refreshments on the coffee table waiting for Sara.

Sitting down on the couch, Sara decided that she had enough waiting. Being patient in situations like this was not in her DNA, and she wanted to get some answers.

"Okay Dad, tell me all about Brie?" Sara grilled him while pouring herself a cup of coffee.

"Brie, as you know, is the lady I met when I went to the travel agency to plan our trip to Italy. She is very nice, full of life, professional and very easy on the eyes," Jon said sheepishly.

Smiling inwardly, Sara continued, "Okay, is she married?"

Jon looked shocked. "No, of course not. She is divorced and has been for several years. Why would you think I would be involved with a married woman?" Jon asked emphatically.

"Well, Dad you are quite a catch, and some women would want to be with you in any way they can, but then I guess you don't get that. Anyway, that's good. Tell me more," Sara said lightly.

"Not much else to tell. You can make up your own mind when we have dinner with Brie tonight," Jon said with authority.

"Okay, Dad, and that sounds good, but would you tell me what it is you like about her?" Sara asked directly.

"That's a fair question. What I like about Brie is that first and foremost she is a happy person and smiles a lot, and it's a beautiful smile. She's smart, takes great care of herself and has a lot of pride. She is caring in every way, and she is stunning and well dressed. Beyond that, I feel she really cares about me and what I do. She is non-judgmental; she accepts me for who I am and expresses no interest in changing me in any way, at least so far. Does that answer your question?" Jon asked with a big grin.

"Yes it certainly does. She sounds perfect for you, and I am happy for you as well," Sara beamed happily.

"Honey, I have no idea where this is going, but, for now, I am enjoying finding out, and I think she is, too. I am too old to worry about too far down the road. My focus is on enjoying each day as it comes." Jon said seriously. "Is that selfish of me?"

"Not at all dad. In my mind, you've earned the right to have some happiness. I know you have mourned Mom all these years and that is not what I believe she would have wanted, so I'm glad you can move on after all this time." Sara reached for his gentle hand.

"Sara, I will never forget your mother. No doubt she was the love of my life. She put up with me for years after Nam, and that was not easy. She was a saint in my mind but now, at this point in my life, I need someone to share my days with, and hopefully some nights as well," he said with a boyish grin.

"I know dad, and I believe that with all of my heart. I support whatever you choose, any time, any place, and I always will." Sara said with tears in her eyes.

"I know you do darling, I have always been able to count on you, and for that, I am very grateful. For years it was just the two of us, and I always felt like we had each other's back but I am sure you have some memories of me that most likely were not always positive, no matter how hard I tried," Jon said guiltily.

He rose from the couch. "I need to get myself together. We have reservations for dinner tonight just the three of us. I am so anxious for you and Brie to meet. I know she has been looking forward to this for a while now," Jon said, heading down the hall to his bedroom.

"Dad, while you are getting ready do you mind if I go into the attic and poke around? I would like to look for more photos that I can add to that amazing scrapbook you gave me for Christmas," Sara called out.

Jon responded, "Look for anything you like. But do not bring any of my baby pictures to dinner with you, okay?" he warned in a forceful tone.

Sara went up the stairs to the attic, and when the light came on, she was astonished at the amount of stuff stored there. Apparently, he had not thrown anything away in a very long time.

She spotted a chest in the corner and thought it looked like as right a place to start as any. Opening the chest, she felt almost like she was violating her father's past to some degree, even though she knew this was her past as well.

Digging down into the pile of papers, albums, and shoeboxes filled with the unknown she came upon a box that indeed had not been disturbed for years. The printing on the shoebox was faded and discolored, but she could still see that it was a box that at one time held her baby shoes. She could make out the size, three, so no doubt she was an infant. Two things were amazing to her. First, the name of the shoes was Stride-Rite, and the cost was $9.50. How times had changed, she said to herself with a smile, remembering the price of her shoes for the Evans Christmas party.

Taking off the lid she discovered the box was full of old photographs. Many were just the usual family gatherings, what appeared to be a vacation or two that she did not remember. Then she found a handful of photos of her mom and dad. She had seen most of the pictures of her mom at some point over the years, but not these of her father.

She couldn't help but notice how sad and cold he looked. There was not a single picture of him with a smile. On the back of the photos were dates in 1969 and 1971 and even a few into the late seventies. Back then he had seemed very withdrawn and unhappy for sure. Sara couldn't help notice that even photos of dad and her mom together showed no emotions or signs of affection. In spite of what she was looking at she had memories of her dad being very affectionate with both of them, so somehow things had changed in later years.

She also remembered very clearly his pain and suffering when Mom died. This surely seemed to be a clue to his past and his struggles in those years. Sara began to wonder if someone or something changed him and what or who it was that had a positive effect on her father.

That would be interesting to know, not that she ever would.

While looking at the pictures, Sara began to think that most or maybe even all men were changed by their experiences in war, and some were able to move on, and others were not. The real question became, what was it that made the difference? After all, it was indeed logical that people were changed by traumatic events. She had seen examples of that many times in her law career.

A moment later she heard Jon calling her, and she made a mental note that she would get back up into the attic to look for some additional clues before she headed back to the city. It seemed crazy since she really did not know what she was looking for, but her inquisitive mind and desire to help Dad was her driving force, and that was impossible to resist.

When she arrived at the bottom of the stairs, Dad was standing there with a suit and tie on and looked a bit like he was going to a funeral or a prom and she wasn't sure which.

"Dad, You didn't tell me this was a formal evening. I need to change my clothes. Give me five minutes, okay?"

Sara didn't bother waiting for an answer and hurried back upstairs to her room to break out of her travel clothes. Laughing, she thought to herself how cute and sweet her dad looked, all dressed up, and of course, his shoes had the spit shine of a Marine. No surprise there.

Leaving the house, Jon told Sara that Brie had just called and she was leaving late from work and would meet them at the restaurant.

Driving through the small town, Brie could see that very little had changed and somehow that was comforting. "Dad," Sara asked suddenly, "I know you have seen your Doctor recently, right? What's new? Any changes or concerns? How are you feeling?"

"Damn Girl!" Jon exclaimed, "That's a lot of questions. To answer all of them: Yes, I have seen the Doc and not a whole lot new. We can talk about all that crap later. Okay? Let's focus on me having my date with two amazing and beautiful women. This hasn't happened to me for a very long time." He smiled and patted her hand.

The restaurant was crowded and somewhat noisy, but the table they were shown to was near the back of the main room in a rather quiet location and very comfortable. Sara realized that some of these old New England restaurants had been around forever and the decor was rarely changed. It was certainly true here. The restaurant featured ornate woodwork on its walls and doors, soft lighting, and comfortable chairs. The servers all wore the obligatory black slacks and white shirts or blouses with long aprons, and from what Sara could tell all of them were very well trained. She felt like she could have been in a New York City dining establishment, except looking at the specials on the blackboard near the entrance they were about half the New York prices.

While she was looking at the menu, she glanced over at Dad and noticed with a smirk that he was about as nervous as a purse-snatcher in court. He kept his eyes locked on the entrance, watching for Brie and was fiddling with his silverware and his tie at the same time.

"Dad, For Pete's sake, relax, she will be here, and everything will be just fine. Don't have a coronary here at the table." Sara said teasingly.

Jon, looking a bit flustered, looked Sara in the eye and asked, "Has anyone told you lately you can be a pain in the ass?"

Sara giggled. "Not and lived to tell about it. Why?"

Before Jon could answer he jumped up and went towards the entrance to greet a lady, obviously Brie. As he escorted her to the table, Sara stood and extended her hand to say hello, but Brie immediately leaned in for a hug and Sara obliged.

"Sara, I am so excited to meet finally you. Your dad brags about you all the time, as he should," Brie said with a genuine smile.

"I'm glad to be here and meet you as well. Dad has told me almost nothing about you," Sara said, with a sharp glance towards Jon.

"That is quite all right. Whatever you want to know I will fill you in. Your Dad is not much for words or explanations as you probably know much better than I do." Brie remarked.

While they browsed the menu Sara studied Brie as best she could without being obvious. Sara thought to herself that her father's leading lady was adorable, dressed very well and had an elegance about her that was disarming. Small talk began, and Sara felt more at ease with Brie minute by minute. Her lawyer senses were not on alert any longer, and in some ways, she thought it would be nice if this were to work out for both of them.

Sara had a lot of questions but did not want their first meeting to seem like a cross-examination, so it was best to keep the conversation light. Besides she was sure there would be many more opportunities to get deeper into who this lady was and what her intentions were. The evening went by quickly. In no time at all they were finishing their dessert and after dinner coffee. It had been a beautiful evening, and one thing in particular was evident; her dad was hooked. Sara noted how he watched Brie and hung on her every word. He was so childlike. Her only concern was would he survive a disappointment if it happened.

On the way home, Jon was quiet, and Sara sensed that he was waiting for her to share her thoughts about the evening.

"Dad, Brie is a lovely lady. I can see why you like her so much. I really am looking forward to getting to know her better, but I didn't want to be pushy tonight." Sara explained.

"Thank you, honey, I really like her a lot, and well I trust her as well, and that's important to me. I knew you would like her or else I would have kept her a secret," Jon said with a smirk.

Sara looked at him and quipped, "Yeah we all know you can keep secrets. Speaking of secrets, what did the doctor's report say?" Sara asked once more.

"Honey, I am drained. Let's talk about that tomorrow?" Jon said, pulling into the driveway. "I'm ready for bed," he claimed.

"Okay dad, I get that, but tomorrow I want the details and no more delays," Sara said firmly.

After locking the big front door, Jon headed down the hall to his room and over his shoulder told Sara, "See you in the morning dear one. Good night and sleep well."

Sara looked at her watch. Only 10:15. Maybe she should get back to the attic for a while. Sara wanted to continue her exploration, but she also wanted to relax a bit, so after changing into her pj's she poured herself a glass of wine that she found in the dining room. She grinned, assuming it might be a leftover from dinner that Dad cooked for Brie. Whatever, she would take it to the attic and look for clues to old mysteries.

Sara decided to go back to the chest she had found earlier and see what was at the bottom. Excavating this large chest was becoming quite an adventure. In the back of her mind, she was concerned about finding something that perhaps might be more than she wanted to know but her lawyer curiosity was in full swing so she pushed onward.

Near the bottom was another shoebox from what must have been a pair of her mother's shoes as the picture showed a pair of high heels. Opening the box, Sara discovered a stack of what seemed to be letters, wrapped in a white silk ribbon. Sara sat staring at the shoebox wondering if this was going too far. Should she read something so personal or was it her birthright, knowing they probably belonged to her Mother?

Sara sat sipping her wine and staring at the white ribbon, keeping the many pages of paper tied together. Did she really want to know what was in there or was this something best left alone? Having a difficult time imagining anything sinister involving her parents she believed at this point that at the very least she would gain some insight to her past as well as new information about her mother, which for one reason or another her father had not shared.

Gently untying the ribbon so as not to tear it, she opened the first letter. After reading a few paragraphs, it was easy to understand they were love letters from her father to her mother, and by the dates, it was well after he came home. The letters were filled with intimate feelings and descriptions of his life at war as well as details on many of his fellow Marines, but nothing earth-shaking yet. Continuing through the stash, she came across one that after reading it multiple times she understood much more about her dad. The letter she had in her hand was sent to her mom in September of 1970 and apparently was written while she was visiting family in Italy.

Dearest Serena,

I know the past two years have been tough on you, and us in general. I have been struggling with my anger issues and my fears about events back in the Nam. You have had to deal with much more than you could have imagined when we met. My memories have ruled my life for too long.

I have been spending a lot of time with my father, and he has helped me work through many issues and now it's time for me to make things right with you. I believe I am ready to move on with my life and build a future for both of us, if you want that. I have no right to expect you to come home to me but if you take a chance on us, I promise never to let you down again.

If you would think making way for us in the future that would be wonderful. You must know how much I love you and need you, but the way I need you today is so different.

I have come miles from where I was, and I know I can make it the rest of the way with you by my side. To answer the central question in your mind: Yes, I do want a family as soon as you are ready. I believe I am ready.

I hope to hear from you soon.

All my love forever,
Jon

Sara sat there with tears running down her cheeks. She had no idea that her parents had split up before they were married. It was a certainty that much was bothering her father all those years and probably was the cause of his having nightmares all those nights when she was so little. He was clearly wracked with guilt and anger. Sara wondered how could anyone carry that burden for so long and so well?

Somehow he had gotten past most of it because he had led a loving and productive life. Somehow her dad had buried most of the pain and decided to move on with his life. She would like to know just how he did that.

Sara decided that she had read enough of the letters and the rest of them were best left alone. If she were to learn anything more, it would have to come from Dad. She glanced at her watch and saw that it was quite late and knew tomorrow would be a full day. She decided she was going to get the truth about dad's health one way or another.

CHAPTER
TWENTY THREE

The night was pitch black. It was virtually impossible to see a man sitting next to you in a foxhole, much less walking past. On this dark and quiet night, the first and second squads of the platoon were on patrol that had been assigned last minute, based on a report that Charlie was trying to take over a village about a two-hour patrol from the main base. The mission was to prevent the movement into the village by setting up an ambush that would hopefully inflict enough damage to persuade Charlie to go elsewhere. The ambush spot was chosen by the Company Commander and his staff based on intelligence from G2, the intelligence group of the battalion.

Jon never had a high degree of confidence in this source before and had no reason to believe the intelligence now. He put Roselli on point, and he positioned himself in the middle of the line of Marines where he should be and had one heavy weapon in front of himself with the radioman next in line behind him. All movement was to be silent so hand signals would be necessary, except it was too damned dark for that to work. A touch from one man to the next was the only communication that could work at the moment.

The way to the ambush location was dotted with several rice paddies. Crossing them required walking on the dikes between them, which meant they had zero concealment options.

The first squad was about halfway across the paddy dike when suddenly a flare went up and lit up the entire area. As the exposed men dove into the water on each side red tracers came at them from the right line of jungle bordering the paddy.

It didn't take more than a split second for Jon to realize their directed route would take them into the middle of an ambush. Jon froze the second squad in place and moved forward to get a better idea of the situation. The first squad was pinned down pretty bad and really had no escape. Jon knew they were lucky Charlie didn't wait until the whole patrol was on the dikes.

Getting back to the second squad Jon decided to divide his force and try to flank the enemy while they were busy. He felt confident that Charlie did not know they were even there. He sent one group of six to the right into the jungle, with the hopes of making them turn their fire towards them, which should allow the pinned down squad a chance to attack from the front. The first squad had begun firing back from behind the dikes as best they could but for the most part they were firing blind.

The standard response would have been to charge straight into the enemy to disrupt them but they were too few men according to the amount of fire they were taking, and Roselli, the point man knew the second squad would be responding fast.

Jon decided that he needed to get to the first squad and provide some suppressing fire to help them out. He picked up the M60 machine gun that was left by the heavy weapons Marine that he had given his rifle to for the flanking movement.

Moving as quietly as possible through the border jungle, Jon found a spot of slightly high ground and began laying fire down into Charlie. He knew he had limited ammunition, but he expected that the second squad would put an end to the firing from the enemy.

It was well known that heavy weapons Marines were a significant target and once he opened up, he could expect they would throw most anything at him. He did not worry that Charlie had mortars for this ambush but would soon find out if they did or not. After putting a couple hundred rounds into the jungle border Charlie had not let up the surpassing fire against the first squad.

Jon decided the only way to get Charlie to stop firing at the first squad was to give them something serious to focus on. He got up and grabbed the M-60 and charged the enemy positions while firing short bursts of the M60 to avoid overheating the barrel. Just as he climbed onto the last dike in the paddy, his world went black.

Jon passed in and out of consciousness in the chopper and three days later woke up on the Hospital ship S.S. Repose in Da Nang harbor. When his head cleared, and the pain had been dealt with by morphine, he wanted to know how he got there and what happened. The doctors and nurses all told him the same thing. They did not have any answers. The only people that did were still back wherever he came from. They did say to him that his wounds were from shrapnel and that he would recover just fine.

He would scream and beg, "What happened to my men? Are they alive?"

No one could tell him.

Jon awoke with a start and sat up as usual. "This dream will never leave me," he said aloud in frustration and even anger. "How the hell is it that I can only remember so much?"

Jon looked at the clock. 6:15 and he remembered that Sara was in the house and today they would spend the day together. He quickly recalled that she was going to be expecting details about his health. Heading to the shower, he said to himself, *I need to practice what I am going to say to her. If I don't tell her everything, she will be upset later. No way around this.*

He turned the hot water on and stepped into the shower and felt the sting of the spray on his back. It felt good. As he washed his body, he felt his hands travel over the scars from so long ago, and every time he did those memories came back to him in full force. Thanks to his dad he had found ways to deal with them and for that he was always grateful.

Sara rolled, over feeling very cozy, snuggled into the warm bed with the comforter that had been on her bed for a very long time. She could make out the sound of the shower running and knew that Dad was up and would be making the coffee shortly. *Should I get up and make the coffee or let Dad. He prefers it much stronger than I do?* Turning over once more Sara decided to stay in bed, knowing her dad was probably looking forward to making coffee for her and after all, it was his house.

Jon whistled a bit as he headed to the kitchen to make the coffee and have it ready when Sara decided to come down. *I will weaken it a bit as she is just not in favor of man-type coffee. Must be all those high priced baristas in the city that she is used to.* Looking out the kitchen window while the coffee brewed he decided he would just tell her exactly what the doctor told him. *I don't think she will go all panicky on me and maybe she and Brie can support each other. I want to make it clear that we will go on and do what we want to do. I need to make her understand that I do not want to be smothered by anyone. In all fairness I will also let her know that I am committed to improving my diet and getting good exercise to help my situation. She needs to know that I will fight to be able to stick around for her and Brie.*

The weather outside was one of those cold and dreary winter days. Only a small amount of snow was left on the ground but looking around he still knew that spring was not really close.

The neighbors were all indoors as best he could tell, and indeed the youngster from across the street was probably still in bed. His thoughts were interrupted by the sound of footsteps on the stairs. Sara came into the kitchen wrapped in a blanket, smiling and as beautiful as ever. Jon thought to himself that Serena was always most beautiful in the early mornings. Sara was just like her.

"Good Morning Dad," Sara said, as she bent to give him a kiss on the cheek.

"Good morning sweetheart, did you sleep well?"

"Not bad at all," Sara said with a smile, "except I am wondering about your health report so can we get that out of the way first thing?" she asked with an earnest look.

"Yes, we can talk honey. Grab your coffee and let's go into the living room. I will start a fire for you," Jon said as he turned and left the kitchen.

The fire began crackling and instantly gave the comfortable room an even better feel and one of normalcy. Sara stared at the flames, waiting for her dad to start his explanation. She was a bit afraid of looking at him for fear of showing too much emotion, which she knew would scare him.

Jon was looking at the fire, she knew as a way of not focusing on Sara either as he began his explanation.

"Well, it's pretty straightforward. I have kidney disease and heart issues as well as Type II Diabetes from Agent Orange. You know I have old wounds, but they are not really part of the equation. The Doc told me that my diabetes has affected my kidneys and caused hypertension. I don't know all the scientific stuff but basically, my organs are slowly fading, and my heart issues put me at risk," Jon explained.

"He did tell me that I can slow down the kidney deterioration with a better diet, but the heart is what it is. I have meds for all of this, and I do take them religiously, but the bottom line is that there are no guarantees. He is pretty confident that my heart issues can be fixed. Some sort of bypass and blood thinners may be necessary at some point. Details to follow but if I choose this path, then our trip to Italy will be postponed for a while. I was so looking forward to it. That's about as simple and honest as I can make it." Jon finished the overview.

Sara was silent and could not look at Jon for fear of losing her composure. She had many questions but was sure he either didn't know or didn't care. She sensed a confident attitude of resolve from him that whatever would happened will happen.

"Dad, are you going to make an effort to take better care of yourself with the diet mainly?" Sara asked, without looking away from the fire.

"Honey, I will do my best I promise you. Brie has offered to educate me on what I should and shouldn't eat, but please understand that at my age change is really difficult," he sighed.

Sara could contain her frustration no longer. "Dad, please excuse the terminology but what you just said is bullshit and you know it. Age is not an excuse for not being willing to make positive changes. I asked you to have a plan, to do just that for me to see. Do you have it?" she asked emphatically.

Jon was silent and could not look her n the eye.

Sara waited and then continued. "I didn't think so. Dammit Dad, I am not ready to lose you. We are not talking about any huge sacrifices here. Just a change in diet and getting some exercise. I need you to be around for a long time yet and I would imagine considering what I saw last night so does Brie," Sara said, letting him have it.

She was close to losing her patience and composure and she knew it. "How do you expect me to explain to a child I might have that their grandfather wasn't willing to work at being around to meet them?" Sara asked with sarcasm.

"Sara, are you pregnant?" Jon asked excitedly.

"No, of course not. I'm talking hypothetically for Christ sakes," Sara said in frustration. "Dad, I want your promise right now that when you are on the mend you will do whatever is necessary to be as healthy as you possibly can. Okay?"

Jon thought for a moment in silence. Looking at Sara with a hurt look in his eyes was breaking Sara's heart. Sara could not control the tears in her eyes, which were from fear almost as much as frustration in her loving but very stubborn father.

"Okay, Sara, I promise to do whatever is necessary, but I am going to need some help in making those changes," he admitted.

"Dad you will have the help. If necessary I will hire a nutritionist to make a plan and train you on how to use it. No more damn excuses, right?" Sara asked. "And about Italy, who cares, we can go another time. You will have the operation without question. I need you," she said through her tears.

"Sara, I will do my best to stick around for a lot longer. I have not shared the heart issues with Brie yet," he told her.

"Dad, We will get through this together," she told him, finally moving away from the fireplace to sit down beside Jon and put her arms around him. They stayed that way for several minutes.

"Does Brie know the rest of the details?" Sara asked

"Yes she does and she was amazing and along for whatever happens," he said.

Sara held her father's hand and decided to change the subject, at least for the moment. "Dad, I was upstairs in the attic late last night and going through an old chest I came upon some letters that I believe Mom had saved," she shared.

"Really? What letters?" Jon asked with a look of surprise.

"Letters you wrote to Mom when she was in Italy. Did you guys break up or something for a while before you were married?" Sara asked.

"You mean to tell me your Mother saved my letters? I never knew that." Jon said with surprise.

"Yes, Dad, the one I read was when you asked her to come back to you and go into the future with you." Sara explained.

Jon was visibly shaken by this, and after a moment said quietly, "Yes, we did."

He explained, "I was in such a bad place when we met. She did her best to understand and deal with my issues, but it came to a point when she simply did not know what to do or how to help me and honestly she couldn't. I was the only one that could. My father helped me to get to a better place. But, believe it or not, most of my mental help came from you."

"Dad, are you serious? How I could help you then?" Sara asked.

"Honey, I was doing quite well, but when you came along, I was suddenly a different man. The first time I looked at your beautiful face and tiny body I knew I had but one direction to go and that was forward. I knew I had to refuse to let my previous life define me for the future. I also knew it would never be completely gone, but I could manage it and live for the people I loved." Jon looked into her tear filled eyes.

"Dad, can I ask you what specifically has tortured you all these years? What is it that has been in the background that's caused you so much pain?" Sara begged.

"Sara, to put it plainly it is unanswered questions. When I was wounded and taken to the hospital ship, I had no memory of the details. I know we were ambushed, but I have no idea about what happened to my men. No one in the hospital could or would tell me any details, and there are no records that I know of. I really want those questions answered. My job was to take care of and lead my men, and I don't know if I did, or if I failed. It has tortured me all these years, and this is the first time I have shared this with anyone."

The tears began to drip off Jon's cheeks. Sara rose from the couch and walked over to the fire to poke it back to life while she collected her thoughts. *This is a gamble she thought. If I tell him about Roselli and his men will he find peace or more pain? What if he wants no part of what they want for him? I guess if the truth will let him have closure then that is the right direction.*

Turning towards Jon, Sara began, "Dad, do you remember a Marine by the name of Roselli?"

"Yes, I most certainly do. How do you know about him? I have never told you. In fact, over the years Roselli has reached out to me occasionally, but in the past I have never wanted to re-connect with him for a couple of reasons. I am somewhat afraid of what he would have to say, and for the most part, I have had serious reservations about bringing the past into my life today. I worked so hard to put it behind me that I am not sure how I would feel reliving it all over again."

"Dad a while ago Mr. Roselli sent me a letter asking about you and I sort of told him when it was right I would ask you about him." If I could arrange a reunion of sorts, and if I was there with you would you like that?" Sara asked seriously.

Sara decided she was not ready yet to let him know about the medal request.

"Sara, I have had a nightmare many, many times over the years. It is one of three that come to me most often, and years ago it was the one that I would wake up screaming from and scare the hell out of your dear mother. It is very frustrating because I can recall it almost the same every time. Nothing changes except sometimes I wake up before I get to the end or at least what my mind tells me is the end."

Jon's tone was sad and full of pain as he continued. "Honey, part of me wants to say hell yes. However, a deep down part of me is afraid of the answers. But I also know that the only way to deal with the past is to shine a light on it. So yes, if you can arrange it I am willing to try." Jon said with a thumbs-up.

"Don't worry, Dad, one step at a time and I will be with you." Sara assured him.

Sara looked carefully at her Dad perhaps for the first time in a long time. She had a sense that he was afraid and she was equally sure she had never seen that look before. This was not going to be painless she realized, but she hoped that in the end, he would find the peace he deserved.

"Dad, can I ask you a question if you feel like answering?"

"Of course honey, you can ask me anything," Jon replied.

"Why did you join the Marine Corps in the first place? I know you weren't drafted. What was it in your life that led you to the Marine Corps? I don't remember ever talking about that with you or even Mom."

"Honey, I guess the reasons are many. At the time my world was a much less complicated world, or at least now it definitely seems like it was. I was raised by two parents who were hardworking, honest people. Our world consisted of simple ideas like home, family, and country. As a youngster in school, we were taught that our country was the best and always in the right no matter what. We were expected to honor our flag and learn the history that was so important to our way of life. We went to school, came home for dinner and did our homework and on certain nights watched TV shows that were simple, fun and projected the perfect way of life, or at least what the advertisers wanted us to believe.

"We were not aware of problems around the world that other societies were dealing with. As American youngsters, we lived in our bubble, protected from the rest of the world. We didn't have the worldwide news programs and communications that we do today. When space exploration came along, we believed we could beat anyone, and we did.

"I was raised to know and understand the patriotic music, and that loyalty to our government was our duty. I don't ever remember questioning our President or other politicians. Perhaps my parents did quietly, but if they did, it was behind closed doors. My earliest recollection of anything political was the 'I Like Ike' button my father let me wear to school, and I am sure I had no idea who or what he stood for except that my father said he was a good man. I do recall that Dad and Mom were happy when Eisenhower was elected. I grew up with Roy Rogers and the Mickey Mouse Club. My first celebrity crush was Annette Funicello, probably because she was the only girl on the show that needed a bra." He laughed then said, "Sorry!"

Jon continued. "My heroes those innocent days were Davy Crockett, Daniel Boone and perhaps Marshall

Dillon. We didn't have any political activists back then that I knew about, because in our small town we only got two TV channels and that was not every night depending on the weather. Newspapers were delivered by the newspaper guy in his Jeep when we could afford the subscription. Today, world news is instantaneous, and it is often dissected by many several times a day. Our entertainment was radio only in my younger years, and then TV came along, but we didn't have one for a long time.

"Growing up I had zero interest in politics. I was too busy working on the farm next door or working at other odd jobs around the small town I lived in. Even through high school playing in the high school band, I was enthralled with the patriotic music of John Phillip Sousa. The idea of marching in a uniform was the main reason I put up with trumpet lessons in those early years. I remember seeing old photographs of my father in his Marine uniform from WWII and knew early on that I would do the same. Keep in mind that when I joined there was no war going on, at least that we knew about.

"Being raised to believe in America and what we stood for, including the fantastic way of life enjoyed by so many, you were expected to do your part in the military. Besides at the time for me it was also a way to get out of the small town and see something of the world. It was a chance to be on my own to some degree and to experience life outside my little town bubble.

"If you can believe this, I had never met any people of color until I joined the Corps and that was in boot camp at Parris Island. Joining the Marines for me was the logical next step. I knew I was not ready for more school. I needed something more important to do.

"My parents had given me a great gift, but it was also a gift that led me down some less than wise paths in my life. They had gifted me with a significant amount of self-confidence. That gift gave me both strength and weakness, for often I have believed I could do anything I chose to do. Keep in mind that even when I got my orders to Viet Nam, the destination did not say Viet Nam. They read only a permanent change of duty station to Okinawa Marine Corps Base. It wasn't until we reached Okinawa that we were told our real destination. Viet Nam then had barely even reached the evening news, so for me, I had no clue. Even in my early years in the Corps at Camp Lejeune, Viet Nam was not a topic of conversation or specific to our training.

"I was quite lucky to have made rank quickly and had enough stripes to avoid some of the hardships of the lower grades, but well, that is a whole other story.

"So, have I bored you sufficiently and answered your question?" Jon asked.

"Yes, Dad, I guess you could say that joining the Marines was a natural progression for you. Apparently, you did not volunteer for Viet Nam then?" Sara asked.

"No I didn't, and I am not sure anyone did in the early years, but perhaps they did." Jon mused.

"Being raised the way I was it probably what made the disappointment in the war so earth-shattering to me. The whole domino theory that if we didn't stop the communists there, it would be somewhere else. As the war progressed, we could see the lies that had been told. We heard about the anti-war issues at home but then coming home to see all the protests and the hatred towards us was very hard to deal with. We were not thought of as heroes. We Vets were treated as if we were criminals or worse. The atmosphere got so hostile that most of us did our best to keep our service a secret in our civilian life. If someone found out we had been there, we were ignored at best and spit on at worst.

"Your grandfather was a member of the VFW back then and when I came home he took me down to the hall and introduced me around. They all said hello but reminded Dad that Viet Nam was a conflict and not a war so I was not welcome as a member. That hurt a lot. Fortunately in later years the VFW saw the error of their ways and changed the policy, but it still was painful. Not that I gave a damn then, but Dad sure did. I seem to recall he resigned at some point shortly after that.

"It was a horrible time in our history as far as I am concerned and one I am not happy to have participated in. I am now and always will be proud to be a Marine. Looking back, I don't think anyone of us was fighting for the government or the politics. We were fighting for each other and to stay alive and to go home. We followed orders of course, but that's how we were raised. Do what is right, and all will be well. That didn't work out to be true for many of us." Jon said sadly.

"I wish I could have really known your parents, my other grandparents. I think I would have loved them very much," Sara responded.

"Honey I know they loved you dearly and would have spoiled you as you grew up." Jon said with a smile.

"How did you deal with coming home being surrounded by hostility? I was looking at some of those photos upstairs, and you seemed so unhappy and sad."

"I know you remember the story about how your mother and I met," Jon said. "Looking back it is incredible that she wanted anything to do with me. When we met, I was still outraged. I had trouble making friends and keeping any relationships going. My dad was the only one I could talk to until I met your Mom. She had a magical way about her with listening without judgment, and her patience level was off the charts. She had reached a breaking point and left me for a long time. At the time that was painful but her doing that contributed to my moving on because I wanted her more than I wanted the past. When you came along, I was almost close to normal. I still had the same nightmares that I do today, but I was able to handle them and understand that I would not let them define me or rule my life.

"Much of the credit for my moving on goes to your Mother. She was amazing. She supported me every day and loved me unconditionally, even when a sane person would have gone screaming from the room. The other half of that credit goes to my father. I came home angry, not just for my wounds but also because I didn't have the answers I needed. I was angry that I didn't have a chance to get some payback I guess, and I also felt guilty at having made it home when I was sure so many others had not." Jon explained.

"My father, as you know, was a WWII combat Vet and had seen much worse and for much longer than I did. When he came home, he was a hero, but instead of enjoying that or trying to leverage that status he and so many others just like him went on with their lives and made a choice to put the war behind them." Jon said proudly.

"My Dad knew what I was going through and spent hours and days listening to me and talking out my feelings and fears. He taught me how to compartmentalize the issues at hand and to focus on what was important, and that was you and your mother.

"Without going into the gory details, it was my father that saved me in many ways. He told me that the past would never leave me and that was okay. It couldn't hurt me, and the dreams were just that, dreams, and had no validity any longer. My job now was to make the best of my life, and when you came along, I knew I had to make it." Jon said with determination.

"Dad, I see so many men your age wearing tee shirts or hats that proclaim some sort of Veteran status, but you never have. Is there a reason you don't? You are certainly entitled to wear anything." Sara wondered aloud.

"I know I am but for me it is just personal and not something I feel the need to brag about or announce to anyone. Those men do have the right to and should if they choose to and I respect that. That choice is just not for me. I have never felt comfortable doing it, that's all," Jon told her.

"Honey there are many levels and kinds of guilt. For me, I was one of the lucky ones. There were many, many men who went through much worse than I did both physically and mentally. My wounds were minimal compared to so many. One of the most difficult issues for me when I came home was the continuous onslaught of TV news about the war. Every damn night I would see newsreels of soldiers and Marines fighting and dying.

"Part of me wanted to be there to help but a bigger part of me was grateful I wasn't and those thoughts brought on heavy guilt. I was constantly angry with my government for putting those young men through that but I couldn't bring myself to get out and join in the anti-war parades and demonstrations and I felt guilty for that too. In some ways I still do.

"I was conflicted in that I felt if I did participate in protests I was insulting the men who were doing the dying. I am sure the boys who fought and died in Khe San for example were not fighting for some moral imperative of their government. They were fighting for each other and to survive and come home. No other reason. In my mind I'm sure that they drew on their anger to get them through the day and night the best they could."

"Perhaps the most hurtful memory is the way the public treated all of us. That is something that I still struggle with today. I know it was long ago but it still hurts. I really don't know if I will ever forgive my country. I sure hope to," Jon explained.

"The persistent dominant demon I have today is the nagging question about what happened and did I let my men down? I really need that answer to be able to put it all behind me once and for all. Somehow I will find a way to deal with the truth, whatever it is. I know that at least Roselli survived but what about all the others." Jon explained.

"Dad, we will find out together. I suspect the answer is positive because I know you. Thank you for sharing so much with me. It does help me understand." Sara said as she moved in to hug her father once more.

"Dad, I am so sorry for raising my voice but your indifference scares me and my fear of losing you unnecessarily brings out the worst in me," she said.

"Honey, That is perfectly fine. It is my fault. Sometimes I just don't think clearly. Keep in mind that I don't have any symptoms except for my blood sugar levels so in many ways I don't feel sick. If I felt ill I would like to think I would pay better attention. The silent killer diseases are difficult to get a handle on."

Sara nodded in understanding and squeezed his hand tightly.

"Sara, as long as we are sort of telling all here I have a question for you," Jon said with a serious tone.

"Okay, Dad. What is it?"

"We have concluded that I am not getting any younger which also means neither are you. I know you have been focused on your career for a very long time and have chosen not to let anything or anyone get in the way of your goals. I am wondering if and when you might be thinking of having a life other than work?" Jon questioned.

Sara smiled. She definitely knew where this was going. She had some things to say but decided to let him finish his thoughts. Now that he was all warmed up she didn't want to stop him.

"I guess what I am getting to is I know I have minded my own business in the past because I have always had faith that you knew what you wanted and how to get it. Lately, I have thought about you and if one day you might have a family and then I might have some grandchildren. Is that possible?" He asked sheepishly, unable to look Sara in the eye.

Sara stayed quiet for a few moments just for effect and then said, "Dad, I am seeing someone, and it is possible that a relationship will develop but for now it's too early to tell."

"Sara, seriously, when did this happen? Who is he? What does he do? Where is he?" Jon asked with palpable excitement.

"Don't get carried away," she warned. "We have only been together a few times, but I really enjoy being with him and he is a good man."

"Okay, that is all very nice but who is he and what does he do?" Asked Jon.

"His name is Devon Platt, and he is a Congressman from New York," Sara told him with enthusiasm.

Jon was quiet for a moment with a look of shock on his face Sara, "A politician, are you serious? What the hell could you possibly have in common with a politician?" Jon asked loudly.

"Dad, we have a lot in common but most importantly as I said he is a good man who is honest and very sincere in his work for his people. He came up the hard way and additionally he is a Veteran." Sara told him.

"And he rides a Harley." She laughed at the look of shock on Jon's face.

"Well, when do I get to meet him? How often are you together?" Jon said, sounding a bit like a nosey father with a teenager daughter.

"Don't worry, I will make that happen when the time is right. Trust me," Sara said.

CHAPTER TWENTY-FOUR

The weekend had gone better than she could have hoped. Sara left the family home with a sense of understanding about her father that she had never honestly had before. Dad introduced her to his new friend Brie, who she had taken an instant liking to and for the first time in many years or perhaps ever, she had an in-depth discussion with her father about himself. They had had many deep conversations over the years but always about some subject other than him. She came away feeling that perhaps for the first time she had an understanding of what was inside him all those years, and the revelations he shared were enormous.

Having Dad share his history like that gave Sara a much clearer understanding of who he was and the why of his life. Now she was on a mission. Sara would reach out to Mr. Roselli and whoever else he still knew and make plans for them to visit her father and just maybe he could once and for all expel his demons.

As always, the train ride home was an excellent opportunity for Sara to solve problems. She would make a list of the tasks necessary and on Monday morning begin the process of helping her father.

Looking out the window of the train the scenery was undoubtedly dismal this time of year. No leaves on the trees, the dirty snow on the sides of the tracks and the early nightfall. All of this would typically be depressing for the trip home, but this time Sara was full of hope and even a bit excited about the future. She knew not everything was rosy by any stretch of the imagination. The news dad shared about his health was undoubtedly less than optimal, but his attitude was comforting, and Sara had high hopes for him to change his life to help his health improve.

In the back of her mind she wondered if, in fact, he had told her the entire story. Was he holding something back in an attempt to protect her from the inevitable? It was indeed possible. Sara made a mental note to reach out to Brie by phone and have a discussion with her. Perhaps he shared more with Brie for whatever reason, and she would be willing to provide more details in confidence.

The train began to slow down as it wound its way through the tunnels into Grand Central Station. Now that Sara was back in the city her thoughts turned to work but also to Devon. She wondered if he was still in Washington or was back in the city. Sara had avoided calling him all weekend for several reasons. First, she did not want to appear to be chasing him and second, she wanted to devote the weekend to her dad. At that moment she realized he had not reached out to her either but recalled he said he would be busy all weekend in DC, so nothing to worry about.

Now, she really needed to press him on the medal petition for Dad. Mr. Roselli would be looking for some answers when she reached out to him, and truth be told Sara had concerns about her father's willingness to accept any recognition without a change of heart about the past.

Sara grabbed a taxi to her brownstone and realized her mood was right. The air was cold, and the conditions were a bit windy. In New York the wind seemed to be stronger as it blew between the tall buildings. The contrast of the noise level between the city and her hometown was incredible. Just being away for a weekend made the return an attack on her senses.

Opening the door to her eighth floor apartment, Sara dropped her luggage in the entry and went to turn up the thermostat to normal. It was chilly in her apartment after the long weekend. The mailbox held two days' mail, and Sara quickly went through it and found nothing of interest.

She went to the bedroom and decided she would grab a nice hot shower and then get under the warm covers of her very comfortable bed, which was so much bigger and better than the one in her old bedroom back home.

Giving her task list a last look she turned out the light and with a smile said, "Good night, Dad."

The familiar alarm started ringing, and Sara was awake instantly. Instead of her usual slow approach to getting out of bed, Sara was up and moving as soon as her feet hit the floor. She felt a new sense of urgency this morning, and it felt good. She knew she would have a busy schedule today in the office, but she would make time to call Mr. Roselli and Devon.

In planning what to say to Mr. Roselli, Sara realized that she would need to explain there was a good chance that her father would not recognize them. Perhaps he had blocked all memory of them somehow. She told herself that she should find out from the VA if this behavior were a form of PTSD or a complex coping mechanism.

Sara arrived at the office and walking through the door she immediately saw Victoria with her essential cup of coffee.

"Good morning Vic," Sara said with a smile.

"Good morning boss. How was your weekend?" Victoria asked, following her into Sara's office.

"Victoria, It was amazing. I have much to do, but it is all good." Sara replied. "Please try to get Congressman Platt on the phone for me?"

"Yes Ma'am," Vic said with a smirk. "Missed him by any chance?"

Sara caught her meaning and responded, "Maybe I did."

While Sara was looking over her calendar for the day her phone rang.

"This is Sara" she spoke.

"Well hello there. How are you?" Devon asked.

Sara warmed to the sound of his voice. "I am great, and I was thinking about you," she said. *Be careful girl; do not sound too eager.*

"I was thinking about you as well. I wanted to call you all weekend, but I know you were on a mission with your dad and I didn't want to interrupt. I hope that is acceptable," Devon said sincerely.

"Devon, of course it is, and I appreciate it very much. It was an extraordinary weekend, and I am anxious to share the details with you if you would like me to," Sara suggested.

"Sara, that would be wonderful."

"Devon, I have to be honest. I'm getting very impatient with this whole process for Dad. It has been a long time and we still have not had any response. Is there anything you can do to move things along? I mean, after all, what the hell is the point of having connections if they don't do you any good?" Sara said in frustration.

"Not a problem. I will reach out to my contact and see where we are. Hopefully I will have more news for you soon."

"Thank you, Devon," she said. "So, when do you want to get together?"

"How about tomorrow evening?" Devon suggested. "I'll be back in town for a few days, and I would like to spend more than a little time with you if possible."

"I do have busy days ahead, but the evenings we can definitely get together. How about tomorrow night at my place for dinner? Can you make it?" she asked, sounding as reserved as possible.

"That would be perfect, I will see you about 8 p.m. if that's comfortable for you."

"That does sound perfect. I am looking forward to it," she replied, feeling like a silly schoolgirl once more. "Good-bye, Devon," she said as she hung up the phone.

Sara replayed the conversation in her mind and was convinced that he was serious about seeing her and spending time with her. She felt that she was more inter-ested than expected. He was very understanding of her weekend and respected her time with her father. That was a big plus for this man, obviously someone who thought of others more than himself. This was a good guy, and maybe it could go somewhere. *Perhaps I will know more at breakfast time,* she thought to herself. *This working on behalf of Dad better not be just a ploy to get into my pants. If it is he will wish he never met me.*

Sara glanced at her watch and was amazed at how fast the time had flown today in the office. Somehow she had worked right through lunch and had meant to call Mr. Roselli long before now.

Dialing his number, she hoped he would answer and most importantly he would want to visit and spend some time with her father.

Sara was relieved when Roselli answered. "Hello, Dominic here," the voice said.

"Is this Mr. Roselli?" Sara asked, not able to recall his first name.

"Yes, it is, who is this? I am not interested in buying anything so if you are selling something hang up now." Dominic replied in an irritated tone of voice.

"Hi Mr. Roselli, This is Sara Milo from New York. Remember me?" She asked.

"Sara, of course I remember you. I have been waiting a long time for your call. How is the Sarge? Is everything okay?" he asked with urgency in his voice.

"Yes, Mr. Roselli, Everything is fine. I have some news to share and a favor to ask." Sara answered.

"Sara, anything you need I am here, but please call me Dominic," He said, now very relaxed and friendly.

"Dominic, I just spent a long weekend with Dad, and I found out a lot of things I did not know, and I think I have a solution to an ancient problem that Dad has been living with for a long time. He shared with me that he has no memory of what happened to him and how he got to the hospital ship. No one there could or would tell him, so in his mind he assumed the worst and thought that he did something that let you and the other men down, and that's why no one would tell him anything."

"Wow, Sara. That is so far from being accurate. First, we had no way to know they took him to a hospital ship. We assumed he was shipped to a hospital, but we couldn't find out anything either as we were stuck in the damn jungle for months after he was choppered out. You have to understand that communications and record keeping was at best minimal back then and often reports were lost in one fashion or another. At least that is what I was told at headquarters in Da Nang when we finally got a chance to try and track him down.

"What can we do and also have you made any progress getting him his medals that he should have?" Dominic asked.

"Okay, first I am working through a Congressman on the petition, and that's a slow process. Second, would you and any of the other men you are in contact with be willing to visit Dad in Massachusetts? Just maybe he will get some peace with your help by talking to you and seeing you," Sara suggested.

"We would be honored but are you sure he really wants to remember? Did you discuss that with him?" Dominic asked.

"He finally told me he remembered your name but the circumstances around when he was wounded and evacuated… he has no recollection. But I do know he wants to remember, and to get answers to the past that have been tormenting him for so long."

"Well, we certainly can fill in the blanks about his wounds and the ambush details," Dominic offered.

"He tells me he dreams about the ambush and even a couple of other battles but his memory stops short, and he is blank after he is wounded. Dad has no recollection of anything after that. He doesn't know who made it out. I am sure that is one of the reasons Dad has chosen not to visit the wall. He's afraid of seeing names he would know. His fear of the truth about what happened is genuine, yet so not like him at all. I have never known Dad to be afraid of anything. I am also quite sure he, like all of you, has his share of survivor guilt," she offered.

"Dominic, the crazy part of all of this is Dad has led a very productive life and has been a fantastic father and husband. I guess he became an expert at compartmentalizing his life and learned to deal with his past." Sara offered.

"Sara, what do you have in mind?" Dominic asked.

"I will arrange a time and date for you to visit. Let me know who else is coming with you, and I will make all the arrangements. I would like to be there, so I need to find some time to get away from the office and the city again," Sara explained.

"That sounds like a good plan," Dominic said. "Let us know, and we will get there. Thank you so much. This means a lot to all of us, and hopefully your dad as well."

"Dominic, I will do that, and I hope to make it very soon. Dad and I have a trip planned to Italy, and I would like this to be all done before that. Are you available sometime in the next three weeks?" Sara asked.

"I will make damn sure we are available. Count on it," Dominic said with enthusiasm.

"You bet I will, and thank you so much. I can't wait to meet you all. I will call you soon Dominic. Take care," Sara said as she disconnected.

Sara realized the where and when would be the next issue. Maybe Brie would have some suggestions and would like to help put this together. She would reach out to her tomorrow.

Sara grabbed her coat and turned out the light on her desk. Looking out of her office it was clear she was the only one left as Victoria had gone home quite some time ago. As Sara left the building the normal street sounds of the city were in full roar and somehow it was almost comforting.

One of the many things Sara loved about the city is that it was always alive and busy. It didn't matter what time, day or night, the city was still alive. Deciding to take a cab home she stepped to the curb, and as always one pulled right up to her. Climbing in she chuckled to her self. It was a known fact that tall, attractive women could get a cab faster than anyone. Did every cabbie hope to get lucky or is it that they were confident they would get paid and not be robbed?

Knowing some cabbies, probably both. Either way, it was a chance to sit back, and just people watch during the ride to her apartment. She could see everything from the homeless to wealthy people. Perhaps because of recent events, for the first time she noticed how many men appeared to be Vets, either homeless or needing help.

Clearly, those needing help came from all sorts of backgrounds, and she made a promise to herself that once she had her father taken care of, she would find a way to help Veterans and the organizations that supported them. Tonight it was easy to see that the holidays had passed and the store windows were getting back to normal and she could sense a bit of a letdown by the inhabitants of this metropolis.

What she was most amused by was how most everyone was back to being on a mission of their own. Quite often people did not even notice others or even acknowledge each other as they did during the holidays. Many walked right past people in need or even people in distress. Yet as a whole, the city dwellers were a tight-knit group for sure, especially since 9/11. It was true that anyone could find anything they were looking for somewhere in this giant city. If only the holiday attitudes could be permanent all year.

Sara woke a bit earlier than usual, perhaps because of her anticipation for her date with Devon. Climbing out of bed on a chilly winter morning had never been one of Sara's favorite chores but certainly necessary to start her day. She also knew that her day would be a busy one Now that the holidays had passed, the courts were back on normal schedule and she had several cases to deal with.

Sara was walking to the shower when her phone rang on her nightstand. Seeing the caller ID she did not recognize the number and was inclined to ignore it but the area code was her dad's Massachusetts area code so she answered.

"This is Sara Milo, who is calling please?" She asked, sounding rather annoyed.

"Hi Sara, this is Brie, your father's friend if you remember."

"Brie, yes of course I do. Is something wrong with Dad?" The room grew colder as she waited for an answer.

"Well, there is a problem, yes. He was feeling rather tired last night and in the middle of the night he called me and I picked him up and we are now at the VA Hospital in West Roxbury at the cardiac unit."

"Brie, what is it?" Sara asked, now in a panic.

"His doctor told me a few minutes ago that they will be admitting him and getting him ready for by-pass surgery. He has two major blockages. They also told me they are confident he will be fine. That is about all the details I've been given so far. They plan to operate this afternoon as soon as they can make all of the arrangements. He's stable right now and talking, and of course complaining a bit. He told me not to call you but, well . . ." she trailed off.

"Brie, thank you for not listening to him. I am on my way. I should be there in about three hours. How are you? Are you okay?" Sara asked

"Yes, I'm fine. A bit nervous but I believe all will be fine. I will be here waiting for you and we can go to his room together if you like," Brie offered.

"That sounds good. Thank you so much again. I will get there as quickly as I can," Sara promised.

"Sara please be safe, it's not critical at this point."

"See you soon Brie." Sara said, hanging up.

Sara decided against the shower, she could do that at her dad's house. She needed to get there, fast.

Flying out the door and to the street Sara grabbed a cab and headed to her office. She called Victoria in and told her she needed a car to get her to Boston as quickly as possible. Victoria didn't take time to ask any questions and left to make the call.

The ride seemed to take forever but Sara knew that the driver did the best he could and drove safely. Taking the elevator to the waiting room, Sara found Brie sitting and reading.

"Brie, where is he? Can we see him?" she asked, during the mutual hug. "I want to talk to his doctor. Do you know if he is available?" Sara asked urgently.

"Yes he is available. He asked me to let the nurse know when you arrived. I'll go do that," Brie said as she hurried down the corridor to the nurses' station.

Sara took a moment to look around. In spite of the government look to the building there was a certain comfort about this place. Clearly people who cared did some decorating to make it look more friendly and inviting. Sara saw a man in a white coat headed her way and she couldn't help but notice his military demeanor. Certainly not what she expected, a tall good-looking man with a very confident air about him as he approached her.

"Are you Sara Milo?" he asked, extending his hand to meet her.

"Yes I am Sara, and you are Dr. Wilson? Doctor, what is happening with my father? Is he going to be okay? What can you tell me?"

"Sara, Your father has blockages in a couple of arteries and we will determine shortly as to what extent. The cardiac team will be reviewing the pictures and will make the necessary arrangements and determine the treatment. I can tell you what we see so far is very encouraging in that he is strong and should handle the surgery just fine," Dr. Wilson assured Sara.

"There will be about a six week recovery time but the procedures are quite common. Here at this cardiac unit we have a state-of-the-art heart lung machine that offers a unique cardiopulmonary bypass circuit that is coated with heparin, and bottom line is we have significantly less blood loss and fewer complications post surgery. Please try not to worry, the team is uniquely experienced and everything that can be done is being done for the Sergeant. He is quite a guy."

Sara tried to take it all in and hear most of it, but was feeling much more confident now.

"Thank you, Doctor. I appreciate you taking the time to talk to me. I will be here waiting, so please let me know anything you know when you know," Sara pleaded. She knew she sounded like she was talking gibberish as her nerves had taken over.

"Doctor can we see him before you take him?" Sara pleaded.

"Yes, but please only for a few minutes. We have already given him a sedative to keep him calm, not that he needs it. Only a precaution. He's doing just fine."

"Thank you so much again, Doctor," Sara said as she and Brie headed to Jon's room.

Walking down the hall Sara had the strange feeling that this was all eerily familiar. She recalled the last time she was in a hospital for her mom, shortly before she passed away. *This can't be happening again,* she thought, holding back tears. *I need to stay strong for Dad.*

"Hi Dad," Sara said as she walked into his room. "How are you doing?"

Jon opened his eyes and looked surprised but also very pleased to see her. "Sara! What are you doing here? I asked Brie not to call you," Jon said with sadness.

"Well Dad, that was a dumb thing to do. Why don't you want me here?" Sara asked him sternly.

"I do sweetie, sorry. I just didn't want you to worry or take more time away from your work. The doctor tells me it is all a very common procedure and I will be fine and really better that ever. Of course I know that's bullshit but its okay," Jon lied.

"However there is one bad part to all of this. Italy will have to be postponed. They won't let me fly for six months after rehab," Jon told them sadly.

"Dad, Italy can wait. Your health can't so please do what they tell you and we will get through this together." Reaching for Brie's hand Sara added, "all of us together."

"I will sweetie," Jon promised.

"Dad we will be here when you come back to recovery from the operation. See you soon. All my love always," Sara whispered as she hugged him as best she could in the bed.

Before Brie could turn away Jon reached out and pulled her toward him and whispered softly "I love you. Just want you to know that before they put me under," he said with a devilish smile.

Jon waved and winked at both Brie and Sara right after Brie gave him a big kiss that seemed to lift his mood.

"Save me more of those, dear lady." Jon said, grinning in spite of his weak condition.

Sara and Brie left and walked down the hall to the waiting room and both were quiet with their own thoughts for the moment.

Sara was the first to speak. "Dad is going to need someone looking after him for a while. Would you be willing to help me find a caretaker for him in his home? Because I guarantee you he will not stay a day longer in the hospital than absolutely necessary."

"Sara I'm sure you're right, but if it's okay with you I will be that person. I can work from home as much as necessary and be available to tend to his needs. It may seem a bit unusual since we haven't been together very long but I will tell you something that I have not told him. I love him to pieces. He is the most gentle and honest man I have ever known and he makes me feel amazing. He just told me he loved me but maybe that was the drugs talking. I just can't see anyone else taking care of him. If we need medical help they can come as needed, but I will stay in your room if that's okay?" Brie asked.

Sara was quiet for a moment, thinking about how to respond to this outpouring. After what seemed a long time she smiled and looked right at Brie.

"Brie, I am in awe of the chance meeting that brought you two together but so grateful my father has found you and you him. You can do whatever you think would be best for him. I know he will be thrilled, as it's easy for me to see he is crazy about you in many ways. It is very easy to see you feel the same way for sure. Any medical help necessary for the recovery and rehab just let me know and I will take care of all the costs. I'll also do my best to get up here on the weekends at least one day a week, hopefully two. Don't hesitate to call me anytime, I'm always available by phone," Sara said.

"Sara, thank you for supporting me and trusting me with your father. I suspect we will make a good team and get our man back to normal. We all have much left to do and enjoy in the future. This will also be a great opportunity to correct his eating habits and help his kidneys as much as possible," Brie offered with a knowing smile.

"Brie, I did not know he shared all of the details with you. He did and you are still here. That's incredible."

"I meant what I said, Sara. I love your father," Brie said. "Not sure how it happened so fast but I do. I probably do not need to mention this but since we have known each other for a very short time I want you to be comfortable with my motives. As an attorney I am sure you think about the details and what's good for your father. It's important to me to be sure you understand that I have no ulterior motives for this relationship. I am not some sort of gold digger that would take advantage of someone like your dad and his situation. I have my own financial resources so I don't need your father for anything other than companionship, love and friendship. I know things like this can be hard to talk about but you are welcome to ask me anything, anytime."

"Brie, to be honest I do not question your motives but I do appreciate you openness. Dad is the kind of man who mostly wears his heart on his sleeve. Fortunately he is very blessed with a lot of common sense and sensible thinking. I don't really worry about him in that regard, just his health."

"Sara, maybe you should stay here to be ready for when he is out of recovery. I would imagine he will be here for a few days but I should go to his house and make some preparations. Like cleaning out the fridge and the pantry of whatever he shouldn't be eating. There is also most likely laundry to do, plus two of us here could be too much for him right after surgery. I'll also make a list of groceries to buy and perhaps you can give me some ideas as to what he will and won't eat. Certainly do not want to treat him like an invalid," Brie said thoughtfully.

"Brie, are you sure you don't want to stay? He'll be looking for you." Sara suggested.

"Sara, just let him know I will be in charge when he goes home, sort of, anyway." Brie said with a smile.

"I will do that, but please come back later as I am sure seeing you will be good for him." Sara said.

"Okay, I'll be back tonight. Call me if anything changes, please." Brie asked.

Once Brie stepped onto the elevator, Sara was alone. She thought that waiting in a hospital waiting room had to be the purest form of torture ever conceived. She felt damned helpless, but somehow she also knew her father was going to make it. He was a tough guy with plenty of reasons to live, not the least of whom was the new, considerate woman in his life.

Sara felt her cell phone in her pocket and for the first time she thought to check emails and messages. She had not felt the buzz but recalled she had turned it off when she arrived at the hospital. Maybe a walk outside would do her good.

Leaving the waiting room she let the on-duty nurse know she would be just outside if she was needed. Walking out the door the sudden fresh air felt exhilarating and once she got past the smoking area the spring air was crisp and a bit chilly.

Taking out her phone she scrolled through the many work emails and found one from Devon. Apparently Victoria had reached out to him to let him know of the sudden trip to Boston and why. Sara was reminded again how brilliant and thoughtful her assistant was, and then realized she'd be missing her date with Devon.

Devon's message was simple and to the point. He knew what was happening and if she needed anything to please call him night or day. *Wow, he is really trying to be there for me. Once I know Dad's in the clear I will call him.*

Sara began walking around the hospital grounds making a point of staying within eyesight of the door in case the nurse came looking. It was a time of reflection about her father and their relationship and that reflection brought so many memories but a few in particular. When her mom passed away he was her rock as they say. He listened, he held her, he cried with her and he also cried alone for many weeks, but he never let her know his pain for he knew she had her own. They spent a lot of time together as her mother would have wanted and their bond was so strong that they both survived the incredible sadness that enveloped them.

As time went on and Sara was able to move forward with her life through the veil of pain and loss she somehow sensed that her dad had not been able to as fully as she had. He never showed any interest in seeking out another relationship for so many years. Now finally he was open and willing to share his life with someone else.

She chided herself that for so many years she had also focused entirely on her education and career, which until recently had been enough for her. Sara realized now that she had been so afraid of any pain that could go along with new relationships that she had avoided any entanglements, either short term or long.

Three hours had gone by, which was about half the estimated time for the procedure. Sara came to fully realize that waiting was not a skill she possessed. In the waiting room she casually glanced through magazines that were truly written for the less serious people of the world.

Suddenly a cup of coffee was offered and when Sara looked up Devon was standing there with the most comforting smile she could remember seeing on anyone.

"Devon, what are you doing here?" Sara asked, shocked.

"Well, I just decided that if you needed me you might not want to call so I decided to get up here to make sure you were okay. I can only imagine how terrible it is to wait alone like this," he explained.

Sara stood and fell into his arms without even thinking about it. His arms closed tight around her and it felt wonderful. Unable to speak, Sara held on tight and after a moment simply said, "Thank you."

Sara gathered herself and broke the embrace and took his hand as they sat down together.

"Do you know anything yet?" Devon asked.

"Only that Dad should be fine and that the operation is a fairly common procedure. The rehab time will be about six weeks so the challenge will be to get him to follow the necessary steps. The good news is he has a new girlfriend and I suspect he will do anything to please her. Her name is Brie and I really like her," Sara told him.

"So for the most part all is looking up?" Asked Devon.

"Let's wait and see the outcome before we start celebrating. I am still scared about all of this and I am really glad you are here." Sara answered.

Sara and Devon went back outside where talking was less intrusive to the others. The mood in the waiting room was indeed somber as one might expect as each of the loved ones waiting all had much to worry about.

Walking along the path towards the garden Devon was the first to speak. "Sara, I know a bit about your dad from our conversations and I do know all about the details of his heroism. What I don't know fully is what he has been dealing with for so long and what effect it has had on him. Can you share the details with me?" Devon asked.

"As you know Dad was in Viet Nam back in the early sixties and that was an early part of the war. The public knowledge then was very little and nothing much was being said when he went there. However, when he came home things were different and continued to get worse as time went on. He felt a tremendous amount of guilt and anger when he came home, just like all of the returning men did. Early on in his return to his life he did not deal with those issues well.

"He now tells me he had what is called today survivor's guilt. He felt guilty for having made it home alive and guilty for so many that didn't. His father helped him enormously and after he and my mother met she helped him as well. To hear him tell it, his healing and ability to move on was really successful when I was born. He told me once he saw me; his life had a direction and purpose. I knew as I was growing up there was something he was holding back on. Whenever the subject of Viet Nam came up either in conversations anywhere or on television he would find a way to change the subject. I never pushed him on it and neither did my Mother as best as I can recall." Sara explained.

"Well what about this request for a medal by his men in his unit? Where does this come from?" Devon asked.

"As it turns out Dad has kept his personal secret for a long time and it involves this incident you know about. As he explains it, when he was wounded and taken to the hospital ship he was never able to find out how he was wounded and what happened to his men. Those were bad times for records and communication so for all of these years he has harbored the thoughts that no one would tell him because he had failed his men and most or many of them did not come home. Also the same reason he has never visited the Memorial; he's been afraid to see names he would recognize." Sara explained.

"That is a horrible burden for any man," Devon said.

"Yes it is, but particularly a man like Dad who was so courageous and strong all of his life to let the fear of the unknown or unanswered plague him like this. Somehow now he has reached a point in his life that he his determined to get the answers. His goal is to move on as best he can no matter what the answers are. He just recently shared all of this with me.

I'm going to arrange a reunion of sorts between Dad and a couple of his men who you have statements from. They will provide the answers and hopefully release him from his self imposed bondage," Sara explained with pride.

"I suppose there are many men in the same position today, and they also need help dealing with the past. Your dad is lucky to have you and his men to help him through all of this. I am sure the returning Vets of today face many of the same issues." Devon said.

"Yes, I'm sure there are many Vets in the same situation but fortunately America has grown up and no longer hates the soldier. They may hate the war, as they should, but no longer the soldier doing his or her duty. When I get dad settled down after this I plan to devote some of my law practice to helping Vets, Pro Bono, in any way I can. That may include lobbying some politicians like yourself," Sara said with a grin.

"I will stand right beside you in that fight if you will have me," Devon promised.

Just then the nurse called out to Sara from the door to the emergency room. Moving quickly, Sara and Devon went into the hospital.

"Ms. Milo, your father is in recovery and doing well. The doctor is on his way down to talk to you," she explained.

Sara stood in the hall waiting and pacing and Devon just stood by to be there if needed. Doing her best to remain calm Sara saw the doctor coming down the hall and he looked pleased.

"Sara, your dad is fine. Everything went just as planned. We ended up bypassing two main arteries and repaired one valve. This little tune-up should hold him well for many more years. However, I do need to warn you he really needs to pay attention to his diet, not just for his heart but also for his kidneys. I will have strict instructions for his recovery time and habits in the future. Do you think he will cooperate?" Dr. Wilson asked.

"Doctor, first, thank you so much for all you and your staff did for my father. I know he will be grateful and that alone should inspire him to behave but if that is not enough, his lady friend Brie will be an even better reason for him to do what he needs to do. So to answer your question, yes, one way or another he will behave!" Sara promised.

"That's good to hear," the doctor smiled. "The nurse will have all the paperwork and we will keep him here for three or four days depending on the healing and then he can go home and begin his recovery."

With that, Dr. Wilson turned and headed back down the hall and through the double doors.

Sara watched him leave with wonder. "It must be amazing to be able to do what they do and help people continue their lives. That is an incredible gift." Sara mused.

Just then she remembered she had promised to call Brie. "Brie, Dad is fine and in recovery. You can see him in a couple of hours and I will be back to go in with you. Devon is here and I need some food," Sara told her.

Sara could hear Brie sobbing on the other end. She managed to say, "thank you so much for calling." Sara realized dad's new woman was more worried than she let on.

CHAPTER
TWENTY-FIVE

Six days had gone by rather quickly. Sara was back at the hospital; this was the day Jon was to go home.

Sara and Brie decided that Sara would pick him up and Brie would be waiting at the house. Sara needed a bit of time to make sure Dad understood the rules for his health and that she was expecting him to handle the changes well and cooperate with his new housekeeper. Brie and Sara had kept her new role a secret while he was in the hospital. Neither wanted any arguments from him. At first Jon did not understand why he would need a housekeeper and in fact didn't want any strangers in his house every day. Sara assured him it was doctor's orders and hers as well so he'd just have to get used to the idea.

Sara and Jon arrived at the house and when Jon opened the car door he spotted Brie standing on the steps, looking like a million dollars. Jon waved and called out, "I didn't expect to see you today."

"And why not?" Sara asked.

"I was hoping but not expecting. I figured you were working," he said.

Moving slowly up the steps to the house Jon walked in and became instantly aware of the female touch that had taken place. Flowers, clean floors, clean windows. For a brief moment Jon wondered if this was his house. It even smelled nice and fresh, he thought.

As the ladies helped Jon to his bed he asked, "Who is the housekeeper and where is she? When do I get to meet her?" he asked.

"She's right here," Brie said, pointing to herself with a wonderful smile.

"So we get to play house? Really?" Jon asked in a devilish sort of way.

"You get to recover and I get to take care of you and see that you obey the rules. That is all for now." Brie bent over to give him a quick kiss.

Sara watched all of the back and forth and finally asked, "So, Dad, what do you think? Will this work for you?"

Jon was quiet for a moment and looked at them both. With tears suddenly pouring from his eyes, he just nodded. At last he spoke, "Don't you two know I just had open heart surgery and you do all of this to get me excited? Thank you, I love you both," he muttered.

For the next month Sara was only able to get up to Boston for Saturday and part of Sunday each week but she quickly observed her father was better and better with each visit. Looking in the refrigerator and pantry it was easy to see Brie was in charge and all was well. She was quite confident that the time to put together the reunion was fast approaching. She decided to bring up the subject and make plans for Roselli and the others to visit right after the six-week rehab period, which was now just two weeks away.

"Dad, you recall our discussion about a reunion with some of the men from your unit in Viet Nam?" Sara asked.

"Of course I do, when are we doing this?" He asked.

"If it's okay with you and they're available I am thinking in a couple weeks. I will make plans to spend a long weekend here to be with you if that's okay?" Sara asked

"Honey, two weeks sounds just about right," he said. "Of course, I want you both here, at least in the beginning. I will trust your judgment on that."

Brie spoke. "Jon, Sara has shared with me much of what you have told her. I guess she thinks I need to know to be prepared. I just want you to know that we will get through this together, whatever it takes."

Another weekend had come and gone and Sara was on her way home. She reminded herself to call Roselli first thing in the morning and find out if two weeks would work for them. She also needed to know who was coming and also from where they would be traveling. She would give the info to Victoria and let her make the arrangements for the travel and hotels nearby. She knew this was going to be an emotional time for her dad and her main concern was his health. She had cleared the activity with the doctor. He even suggested that it would be good for him. His vitals were strong from the last examination so he did not have any concerns.

The last four weeks had been a crazy time and she hadn't had much time for Devon between work and running up to Boston on the weekends. They did chat on the phone regularly and she was so impressed with his patience and sincere concern. *Once this is over I am definitely going to spoil that man.*

Two weeks flew by for most, but not for Jon. He was dealing with a bunch of mixed emotions. He was excited to see his men, fearful of what they might say, and he realized that most likely he would not recognize anyone. He was relieved and gratified that after all of the years he was dealing with his nightmares and secrets it was time to face them head on. He would be forever grateful to his amazing daughter for her support and love. He asked the universe how he got so lucky.

His only regret was one not in his control. He wished his Serena were here but he had thought on more than one occasion that she had somehow sent Brie to watch over him and love him. He knew that was certainly far-fetched but nonetheless it was quite comforting. Jon laughed at himself and was convinced he watched too many Hallmark Channel movies. It was only recently his anger towards the politics that had put so many men in harm's way so long ago had subsided. Sadly he felt the government was repeating that history and had learned almost nothing from the horror, stupidity and greed that had perpetrated Viet Nam.

Jon looked at his watch and knew it would be soon that Roselli, Watkins and Konkel would be arriving. He did remember Roselli for sure but honestly had no real solid recollection of the other two names. He had great hope that he would recognize them on sight or at the least as they recalled their times together.

He had to believe that if they were coming to see him then whatever happened they must have forgiven him or at least did not blame him. If he did something wrong his sincere hope was that they would forgive him and believe that he did his best at that time.

Looking out the window he saw a large SUV limo coming closer and he knew it was Sara and the men. Sara couldn't just take a couple of taxis; she had to do it up right. Must be the way they did things in the big city. Amazing girl, he thought for a moment, half country girl and half city slicker, certainly the best of both worlds.

Watching the men exit the vehicle he was not able to tell who was who. He suspected Roselli was the big guy with the full head of gray hair. He also seemed to be the leader of the group and they organized themselves to walk up the path to the house with Sara leading the way.

The door opened and Sara entered first.

"Dad, I want you to meet again, Corporal Dominic Roselli."

Roselli crossed the room with the grace of a man on a mission and not a word was said as the two men embraced each other and the tears began to flow. They stood together in that embrace for several moments without any words as the pent up emotions of both Marines flowed from their pained memories. Only men who had been through hell together could possibly understand the deep and forever bonding feelings that they were both experiencing.

Breaking the embrace but still holding each other at arm's length, Roselli broke the silence.

"Hi, Sarge, Damn you are old but it sure is good to see you once more," he bellowed.

Jon laughed through his tears and slapped Roselli on the shoulder. "I see you still don't have any respect for rank. I may be old but man, you are fat," Jon countered.

The ball-busting remarks put everything on a normal playing field for both men. It relieved some of the expected tension and took them back over time to when they were both young Marines.

Jon looked past Roselli and took in the looks of the other two men. Mike Watkins stepped forward and extended his hand to Jon. Jon pulled the man into him for a hug without saying a word. Breaking away Watkins told Jon, "Sarge, I don't think you will remember me very well. I was only in your outfit about two weeks before you were taken out. However, I sure remember what you did for me."

Jon was so focused on the introduction he missed the reference to his actions by Watkins.

"Mike, you are right. My memories of those times are damn foggy but I'm sure glad you made it home to be here with us today," Jon said very sincerely.

As Watkins stepped aside Konkel moved toward Jon with his hand out and Jon did recognize him once he spoke.

"Jesus Christ, you were my radio man!" Jon said very loudly. "Nathan, I thought for sure your name would be one I would see if I went to the wall. Damn, it's wonderful to see you. Hell, it's damn good to see you all.

"Sorry but I'm still recovering from some plumbing work they did on me." Jon explained. Please come in and sit down we have a lot to talk about. I would assume you all know my daughter Sara by now. I need to know what you have been doing since the last time I saw you, if you want to tell me that is." He preferred to put off the questions he really wanted to ask.

"Sarge, we can get to all the normal crap of life later. We all came this far to answer questions that have been plaguing you for so long, according to Sara anyway. If you can, why don't you tell us what you remember before you were choppered out." Roselli suggested.

Jon took a long moment and then began to relate the painful memory. "Dominic, what I remember isn't much. I remember we walked into an ambush. You and the first squad took a shit storm of fire from the paddy border. I remember the screen of red tracers headed your way. I knew you were pinned down behind the dikes really bad. I sort of remember sending part of the second squad to flank Charlie's positions and I think I recall picking up an M-60 and laying down some fire, then that is about as far as I can take it.

"The next thing I knew I was on the hospital ship bandaged up and full of morphine. I know I asked how

I got there but they either couldn't tell me or wouldn't. Honestly one of the many reasons I am glad you guys came is I hope you can forgive me for letting you down. What I don't know is how many men we lost that night. I have always felt I should have done something different or have done more in some way." Jon finished his recollection and cleared his throat.

Roselli, Watkins and Konkel all looked at each other in disbelief. It took a moment for Roselli to speak.

"Sarge, You have it all wrong. Well, almost all wrong. You are right; we were ambushed. I was on point as usual and Charlie let me walk right by to have more targets. I never sensed they were there and what's even stranger to me is that I never smelled them.

"When they opened fire the squad all dove into the paddy and fortunately Charlie didn't shoot so well in the dark. You were also right; the bastards did have us pinned down pretty bad. I knew you would try to flank them with the second squad so I made everyone stay down and wait.

"Moments later I heard an M60 open up and I knew someone was trying to suppress Charlie's fire. Honestly, at the time I didn't know it was you. You picked that gun up and began to charge the jungle border, which gave us the opportunity to get off our bellies in the mud and move forward, firing as well.

You kept going into the jungle and the only way we could see you was the glow from the hot barrel of that M60. As best we could tell you took out at least five and sent the rest on their way. The ambush was over almost as fast as it had begun. One of the Cong must have thrown a grenade your way because that's what stopped you. When the firing stopped we got to you and put bandages where we could, gave you a morphine injection and called in a chopper. That was the last we saw of you," Roselli explained.

Jon sat in his chair with his mouth open and crying like a little boy. The emotions of all the years left his body all at once. One by one each of the men put a hand on Jon's shoulder to comfort him and connect in a way only men in combat can.

"Sarge, you didn't let us down you saved our sorry asses. Each one of us. You were the only casualty in that mess, except for the G2 Staff Sergeant I punched in the mouth when we got back to camp, for his shitty intel," Roselli finished.

Jon looked across the room at Sara and he could see her tears were also flowing but the look of pride on her face was the best medicine he would ever get.

"Sara, would you call Brie and see if she can join us please?" He asked quietly. "I want her to meet these men, and they her."

The thought that these men might be thinking of him as some sort of hero really became uncomfortable so it was time to change the topic of conversation and lighten things up a bit.

"Okay, enough talking about painful shit. Tell me what you guys have been doing all these years. Roselli, I think by looking at your belt size you must have taken over your family's restaurant," Jon chided.

The stories and details of three lives took two days to share along with great meals, some serious drinking and the rekindling of relationships that only men who have fought together could comprehend. All branches of services had close relationships but the men of the Marine Corps had a brotherhood only understood by the few. To them Semper Fi was not just a Latin slogan meaning Always Faithful; it was a greeting, recognition of a life shared and a promise to live by. From boot camp to grave Marines had a special place in American lives and American history and always would. If forgiveness had been necessary, it would have certainly been given by fellow Marines.

At the end of the reunion Sara could see very plainly that her dad no longer carried the burden of guilt and regret, and for her that was everything. The men would go back to their lives with promises to stay in touch and get together more often. Jon would go back to the process of healing and figuring out how to hold on to Brie for the long haul.

Before the men left Roselli pulled Jon aside and in secret told him as he pointed to Brie, "You are one very lucky jarhead," as he slapped him gently on the back.

CHAPTER
TWENTY-SIX

S ara headed back to New York, leaving her father in Brie's most capable hands. Her witnessing of the reunion fed the fire within to get the recognition her father so clearly deserved. She would do whatever it would take. Devon was certainly on it but she thought there had to be more she could do. She would speak to the other lawyers in her firm and try to find any connections to the decision makers she could. Not that she would use any leverage, as she only wanted this to be authentic, but she did want to speed things up. In spite of the great outcome of her father's recent surgery she still had concerns for his health.

Waking at her usual time, Sara went through her normal routine and decided to go down to the mailbox she ignored on her way home. She hoped some news would be there that would make her day. Opening the box she leafed through the plethora of junk mail and brochures she was once again disappointed. No matter, she was determined to get some answers, and soon.

Normally on such a nice day Sara would walk part of the way to her office, sipping on a latte form the little barista a few doors from her brownstone. Today she grabbed a taxi and was on a mission. Out of the taxi into the elevator and up to the prestigious seventh floor she headed to her office. Victoria saw her coming and could easily tell by her body language she had something big on her mind.

"Good Morning Boss," Victoria said.

"Good Morning Vic. Please get Congressman Platt on the line if you can find him," she answered as she continued quickly into her office.

"Ms. Milo, before I do that, this came for you Friday. You might want to read it before you call the Congressman." Victoria handed Sara an envelope.

Sara took the envelope and read the return address. It was from Headquarters Marine Corps Awards Branch, Washington DC. Sara stared at the package, almost afraid to open it. The fear of being turned down now became palpable. Her mouth went dry and her hands began to tremble. Sara looked at Vic and she took the hint and left the office, closing the door behind her.

Sara walked to her desk and sat down very slowly and put the envelope on the desk. Taking a few moments to gather the courage to find out the answers she reached for her letter opener. *If it is good news I want to keep the envelope in good condition. What a strange thought,* she said to herself and began to laugh.

Okay, big rough tough attorney, open the damned envelope, she admonished herself. Removing the letter Sara began to read. A few words jumped out at her such as "pleased to inform" but the two words that took her breath away were "Silver Star."

"Oh my God," she said aloud. The tears began to flow as she cried almost uncontrollably. *Now what? What comes next?* Sara took a few minutes to get herself together before Vic gently knocked on her door. "Boss, I have the Congressman on hold."

Sara nodded and reached for the phone. "Devon, did they tell you?" Sara asked.

"Tell me what?" He said surprised

"About the medal!" Sara said loudly.

"No, I'm sorry. I haven't heard anything, have you?" Devon asked.

"Devon, a letter was waiting here for me this morn- ing when I came to the office. They approved a Silver Star for dad's action that night," she blurted.

"Darling, that is amazing news." Devon said. "So I guess the question now is, how do you tell your father and when?" Devon asked.

"I've had a plan in my mind for a while if and when this happened." Sara shared. "I would like you to go with me to Boston to see Dad and Brie, and to help me break the news to him. I think it's also time you two meet, and this would be a great occasion considering all the work you put into this as well. Will you do that?" Sara asked.

"Sara, it would be my honor. If he is willing to accept it I would also like to get the press on board for the announcement and ceremony. If possible I would suggest we get the three men who started this to be involved once he agrees. What do you think?" Devon asked.

"Devon that sounds wonderful, but first things first. I have a gut feeling that Dad is going push back on accepting any medals for anything for many reasons. We won't know until we try. I am going to certainly do my best to get him to accept. If he does would you take care of the arrangements with the government? Do they have ceremonies for cases this old or is it just a quick presentation somewhere?" Sara asked.

"I honestly do not know in situations like this, but I will have one of my staff get all the details. When do you want to go?"

"As soon as possible, of course!" Sara replied.

"I will arrange for a town car to pick you up at your apartment tomorrow morning and I will fly into Boston also in the morning. By the time you get there I will be landed and we will drive right to your father's. Does that work?" Devon asked.

"Oh Devon, that is amazing. Are you sure you can get away so unexpectedly?" Sara asked.

"Darling, I will make it happen. See you tomorrow and try to relax a bit." Devon advised.

Sara realized that Devon had called her darling twice in one phone conversation. That was a first. She smiled inwardly, thinking she liked that a lot.

The next morning when the limo arrived Sara had been ready for some time, since before dawn. She hardly slept with the excitement of being able to give her father the news.

During the ride she went over in her mind how she would tell her Dad what this was all about. What reasoning would she use to convince him to accept this honor from his nation and his men? Could he get past the painful history and the negative thoughts that he was not even supposed to be there, and whatever he had done in reality was not for his country but for his fellow Marines?

She guessed he would try to logically say all he did was use his training and instincts to take care of his men. He would have some very serious reasons and he could be stubborn. Sara had to remind herself that it was his decision and that she would honor and respect that decision, no matter what it was.

Arriving at the airport the driver went into the terminal to find the Congressman. Shortly after they walked out and Devon climbed in beside Sara. Sara just could not resist her multitude of emotions. She reached over and planted a passionate kiss on her handsome prince.

The kiss lasted an embarrassingly long time, given that the driver could not help but see what was going on in the back seat.

"Well now, that's what I call a greeting," Devon exclaimed, as he reached for his handkerchief to remove the lipstick.

"So glad you approve. Soon there will be much more of that I assure you," Sara said with a wink and a smile.

Forty-five minutes later they pulled into the driveway. Sara had told Brie they were coming so she could prepare Dad for the introduction to Devon. She did not tell her about the commendation.

Brie opened the door and greeted Sara with a hug as usual and invited them in. "Dad and Brie, I would like you to meet Devon. Not only is he my significant other now, he is also my Congressman. So Dad, be kind to my politician," Sara begged a little.

Jon stood and walked to them both. After giving Sara a big hug he turned and extended his hand to Devon.

"Welcome to our home and to our family. It's about time she brought you here," he said, grinning at Sara.

"Dad, before we go any further I have some news to share with you." Sara told Jon.

"Am I going to be a grandfather?" Jon asked with a smirk.

"What? No of course not, at least not yet." Sara was obviously flustered.

"Dad, about a year ago Roselli and a couple of others reached out to me for help. They wanted the opportunity to tell their story to the government and had not been able to make any progress. They shared with me the story of your last patrol and what happened and they wanted you to be recognized by everyone else for what you did that night. They wrote statements and provided dates, times and other backup information to request a commendation for you, their platoon Sergeant. Devon helped me put it all together and submitted it to the Department of Defense and the Marine Corps. We have been waiting all this time," Sara explained.

Sara could see her father's breathing was increasing and he looked to have some anxiety over this tale.

"Yesterday, when I went into the office this letter was waiting for me," Sara said showing Jon the envelope.

"To get to the point the Marine Corps is awarding you a Silver Star Medal for your actions on that night and would like to have you accept this award as soon as possible," Sara told him.

Jon fell into his easy chair and sat in silence, obviously stunned by what he was hearing and also trying to collect his thoughts and response.

"Honey, you know I just found out about this a few days ago. Hell, up until then I thought I was failure all of these years. My first thought about this is…bullshit. No one back then could make an effort to tell me the truth and they let me suffer for so long. I didn't do what I did for any medals. I did what my instincts led me to do for my men and no other reason other than to stay alive and go home.

"You know I feel that I should never had been there. In fact, none of us should have. Those feelings haven't changed. I can't accept a medal for participating in such a travesty of a war. Besides, I have always felt the ones that deserve the medals are the ones that never came home. I understand that medals are important but just not for me." Jon's voice grew louder as he spoke.

"But Dad," Sara countered. "You can accept it for your men who want you to have it. It represents the love they have for you and their gratitude. It has nothing to do with the government, particularly the government that was responsible for those times. While it may come from the government, it represents you and your men and the sacrifices you all made. It's not that hard to understand."

"I can see why you are such a good lawyer...Damn." Jon's face was serious as he considered her words.

Sara decided she had said all she needed to say to convince him except for her closing argument. She knelt down beside her father as Brie sat beside him on the arm of the chair. Sara looked directly into his eyes and he returned the steady gaze. It was easy for Sara to see and understand the confusion in his heart and mind. The pain was real and all she could think of saying was...

"Dad, I heard somewhere once... 'Medals are not for what you did...they are for living with it.'"

Jon nodded and let the tears begin to fall as Sara held him close. She whispered in his ear, "Dad, you have so much more living to do. Let this be the ending of that chapter. If you accept the medal I will do my best to give you grandchildren. Deal?"

Sara now knew in her heart that the healing process could truly begin, and she would be there to see him through the process. Jon's tears pulled at her heart but she knew down deep this was a release for him. The future, however long it might be, would be better for them both. Sara could not help being surprised by her sense of relief. She wondered, as her father clung to her, what was in store for all of them. Looking across the room towards Devon and Brie she was comforted in seeing their smiles and suddenly was certain that happy times were ahead.

ACKNOWLEDGEMENTS

I would like to thank my wife Diane for her continued support and encouragement during the writing of this story. Additionally I would like to thank a fellow USMC Veteran and writer Roman Valenti for his contributions and for pushing me to continue on this path when difficulties arose.

Next I would like to thank my daughters Lisa and Jennifer for the inspiration and belief in me to accomplish my goals and their patience for so many years with my past.

Last I would like to thank America for finally understanding and appreciating the value that Veterans offer this country, both past and present and their willingness to help those who need help in so many ways.

It is my fervent hope that one day war will be unnecessary and undesirable for all of mankind.

—Al Hague

BOOK CLUB QUESTIONS

1. What did you enjoy most about A Marine's Daughter?
2. What were your expectations for this book? Did the book fulfill them?
3. Were there any ares of the book that took you by surprise?
4. How realistic was the characterization? Would you want to meet any of the characters? Did you like them? Hate them?
5. Who was your favorite character? Why?
6. Did the actions of the characters seem plausible? Why? Why not?
7. Did you come away with a better understanding of a veterans experience and the emotions veterans deal with upon returning home?

8. Veterans returning from combat missions need support. America's treatment overturning veterans has improved, but what more can we do as a society to embrace those serving our country

9. If you were making a movie of this book, who would you cast?

10. Did the book end the way you expected?

11. What three words would you use to summarize this book?

12. Would you recommend this book to other readers? To your close friend? Why or why not?

GET HELP IF YOU NEED IT

A number of years ago I was diagnosed with Type II Diabetes. In a fluke meeting I met the State Veterans Director and he asked me if I served in Viet Nam? I answered yes I did. He then inquired about my health and when I told him I had recently been diagnosed with Diabetes he told me I was entitled to help from the VA. Long story short my journey with the VA began and fortunately today it is a major part of my life. Most likely the reason I am still alive, able to write this book and see my grand children excel at everything they try.

I was informed that Diabetes and several other illnesses are attributable to Agent Orange exposure in Viet Nam and I was eligible for medical care and financial benefits. The Director made arrangements for me to meet with the American Legion at the VA Hospital in Spokane WA and they assisted me with the paperwork. The whole process went very smoothly with their assistance I received medical care including all prescriptions and benefits.

In 2017 I developed kidney stones and had the necessary procedure to take care of them at a local hospital authorized by the VA. Next came bladder stones that needed to be removed and during that process it was discovered that I had a lesion in the bladder that was malignant. Treatment would be necessary and the presumptive cause approved by Congress was the poisoned water I had consumed when stationed at Camp Lejeune, North Carolina in the sixties. The Bladder Cancer is covered by the VA and additional financial support is provided.

In August of 2018 I had a heart attack caused by Coronary Artery Disease which is an offshoot of the Diabetes which is also covered. Bottom line is anyone of these issues could have been fatal if I had not sought help through the VA.

The point of this story is to tell fellow Veterans that there is help and its not as insurmountable as you might be led to believe. I assure you help is available.

The best place to start is www.ebenefits.va.gov. Here you will find complete information including someone to help you manage the process. It might be your State Dept. for Veterans like mine in Arizona or it could be the American Legion or an advocate at your local VA hospital or clinic.

My personal experience with the VA hospitals and clinics has been extraordinary. The people working there are caring, professional, serious and very pleasant. The respect they show Veterans every day is amazing.

Like any system there are rules. There has to be to avoid chaos and keep the wheels turning. A Veteran can do his part to help the system. For example more than half the appointments made at the large hospital like Phoenix are not kept by the Veteran. That means that time was wasted and someone else who might need the appointment went without. Another observation easy to see is how many vets who do not follow the staff instruction and help themselves by doing the right things. The system, including online, is easy to work with.

While it may seem like a long time to get something accomplished patience is also part of the solution.

There are many organizations offering programs to help Veterans have a higher quality of life but when the

Veteran takes some of the responsibility for his own care, the system works even better.

Here are some additional links to find help you may need.

https://vva.org Viet Nam Veterans of America https://www.legion.org The American Legion

CPSIA information can be obtained
at www.ICGtesting.com
Printed in the USA
LVHW08214912128
600229LV00018B/372/P

9 781642 371185